Everyday Basket Patterns

Step-by-step instructions to make over 150 useful baskets

Copyright © 2023

All rights reserved.

Hardcover KDP ISBN: 9798374923568
Paperback KDP ISBN: 9798374823202

Patterns written by Marj Campbell
Edited and compiled by Janna Camperman
Cover designed by Janna Camperman
Photographs by Marj Campbell

Deuteronomy 28:5

Introduction

My grandma, Marj Campbell taught basketry – and made lots of baskets – at her small-town gift and craft store for many years. During this period, she spent a great deal of time designing and writing patterns for her monthly basket classes. A variety of styles, many of these patterns focus on being practical but beautiful designs that are useful for a myriad of everyday purposes. I recently have desired to begin basket-weaving again and thought of compiling all of my grandma's patterns into a book so that I (and now you) can have them in one place for years to come. She has been and still is a major inspiration for all the creative ventures in my life.

Janna Camperman

Table of Contents

Chapter 1: Basic Baskets

- Berry Basket 8
- Berry Basket with Chicken Feet 9
- Small Berry Basket 10
- Basket with Ribbed Handle 11
- Small Things Basket #1 12
- Small Things Basket #2 13
- Sea Grass Basket #1 14
- Sea Grass Basket #2 15
- Homespun Basket 16
- Hearth Basket 17
- Hearth Basket with Wood Base 18
- Mini Hearth Basket 19
- Clammer Basket 20
- Clammer Basket with Wood Base 21
- Utility Basket 22
- 3 Nested Baskets 23

Chapter 2: Market Baskets

- Market Basket with Wood Bottom 26
- Market Basket with Woven Rim 27
- Fancy Swing-Handle Market Basket 29
- Square-Bottom Market Basket 30
- Herringbone Market Basket 31

Chapter 3: Williamsburg Baskets

- Small Williamsburg Basket 34
- Large Williamsburg Basket 35
- Williamsburg Twill Basket 36
- Williamsburg Tote with Color 37
- Square-Bottom Williamsburg Basket - Small 38
- Square-Bottom Williamsburg Basket - Medium 39
- Square-Bottom Williamsburg Basket – Large 40

Chapter 4: Baskets for Around the House

- Stair Basket 42
- Napkin Basket 43
- Lattice Candle Basket 44
- Tissue Box Basket #1 45
- Tissue Box Basket #2 46
- Cd Holder Basket 47
- Classy Trash Basket #1 48
- Classy Trash Basket #2 49
- Pincushion Basket 50
- Plastic Bag Basket 51
- Lamp Basket 52
- Bathroom Tissue Basket 53
- Pencil Mug 54
- Sewing Basket 55
- Gift Wrap Basket 57

Chapter 5: Plant Baskets

- Plant Basket #1 60
- Plant Basket #2 61
- Small Planter Basket #1 62
- Small Planter Basket #2 63
- Medium Planter Basket 64
- Basket Vase 65
- Round Flower Basket 66

Chapter 6: Food Baskets

- Pie Basket #1 68
- Pie Basket #2 69
- Biscuit Basket 70
- Biscuit Basket with Wood Base 71

Casserole Caddy..................................72
Bread Basket......................................73
Apple Basket......................................74
Large Apple Basket............................75
Double Walled Muffin Basket 76

Chapter 7: Trays

9" X 13" Basket 78
Round Tray Basket............................79
Oblong Tray Basket with Rosewood
   Handles 80
Small Round Tray (12" Or 13") 81

Chapter 8: Storage Baskets

Storage Basket..................................84
Storage Basket with Wood Base................85
Large Storage Basket.........................86
Medium Gathering Basket...................87
Large Gathering Basket......................88
Round Carry-All Basket......................89
Round Carry-All Basket with
   Continuous Weave..........................90
Square-Bottom Carryall Basket 91
Laundry Basket..................................92

Chapter 9: Hanging Baskets

Wall Basket..94
Wall Basket with Wood Base..............96
Plaid Wall Basket...............................97
Weed Basket......................................98
Doorknob Basket................................99

Chapter 10: Purses and Totes

Basket Purse #1................................102
Basket Purse #2................................103
Basket Purse #3................................104
Basket Purse #4................................105
Basket Purse #5................................106
Purse #6 — Lightning Purse................107

Tote/Purse Basket with Leather
   Handles 108
Tote Basket......................................109
Tote Basket with Shaker Tape Handles..... 111
Small Swing-Handle Tote Basket..............112
Hannah's Marriage Basket........................113
Church Supper Basket......................115
Small Twill Flag Tote.........................116
Open Picnic Basket..........................117
Braid and Twill Tote..........................118

Chapter 11: Sectioned Baskets

Utensil Basket...................................120
Small Utensil Basket.........................121
Desk Organizer Basket.....................122
Magazine Basket..............................123
Twill Magazine Basket......................124
Large Magazine Basket....................125
Short/Medium/Tall Divided Basket........126
Divided Craft Basket........................127
Handy Caddy Basket........................128
Flat Caddy Basket............................129
Sarah's Basket..................................130
Weaver's Workbasket.......................131
Tool Basket.......................................132
Peanut Basket..................................133
Jelly Jar Basket.................................134
Picnic Caddy Basket.........................135

Chapter 12: For the Holidays

Easter Basket 138
Stars and s Stripes Basket...............139
Stars and s Stripes Basket with Handle....140
Christmas Basket #1.........................141
Christmas Basket #2.........................142
Santa Basket....................................143

Chapter 13: Using Hoops

Melon Basket 146
Cat Head Basket 147
Potato Basket 148
Melon Basket with Yarn 149

Chapter 14: Decorative Weaving

Diamond Weave Basket...................... 152
Whitecaps Basket............................... 153
Wave Basket 155
Japanese Diamond Bowl.................... 156
Oval Basket with Japanese Diamond Weave 157
Urn Basket... 159
Braided Urn Basket........................... 160
Ridge-Weave Basket.......................... 161
Diamondback Basket 162
Diagonal Weave Basket..................... 164
Zigzag Basket.................................... 165
Flying Geese Basket.......................... 166
Snow-Capped Mountains Basket 167
Bird Nest Basket 169
Little Drummer Boy Basket.............. 170
Blueberry Bucket 171
Spiral Basket 172
Star Swirl Basket.............................. 173

Amish Tray.. 175

Chapter 15: Misc. Baskets

Kettle Basket..................................... 178
Kettle Basket with Wood Base.......... 179
Small Oval Basket with Wire Handle 180
Oval Twill Basket with Wrought Iron Handle.. 181
Large Oval Basket with Wire Handle........ 182
Ribbon Basket................................... 183
Elegant Storage Basket 184
Big Bowl Basket 186
Round Basket with Diagonal Rim..... 187
Round Basket with Double Strand Braided Handle 188
Large Round Basket with Fabric and Notched Handle.............................. 190
Round Gathering Basket 191
Round Gathering Basket with Wood Base.. 192
Beaded Basket 193
Oval Basket with Beads 194
Multi-Color Bowl Basket 195
Pitcher Basket #1 196
Pitcher Basket #2 197
Bowl Basket...................................... 198
Small Pitcher Basket........................ 199

Abbreviations used throughout this book:

FF – Flat-Flat   FO – Flat-Oval

Note on wood base measurements:

As these patterns were written over several years, the sizes of some of the wood bases, mostly the divided ones, were not available. I have included these patterns for inspiration but some inferences may need to be drawn on the exact measurements of the bases.

Chapter 1: Basic Baskets

Berry Basket

Materials:
¼" FF reed
¼" FF reed dyed
3/8" FF reed
½" FF reed
5/8" FF reed
sea grass

Cutting:
4 fillers of 3/8" reed 7" long
5 stakes of 5/8" FF reed 18" long
5 stakes of 5/8" FF reed 20" long
1 handle of 5/8" FF reed 22" long

Weaving:
1. Lay the five 20" stakes horizontally with rough sides up.
2. Weave one of the 18" stakes in the center of the 20" stakes weaving under, over, under, over, under.
3. Weave two stakes on each side of the center stake
4. Weave in fillers weaving same as 2nd and 4th stakes. Base should be 5" x 7".
5. Bend stakes up.
6. Weave 3 rows of ½" reed.
7. Weave 3 rows of ¼" dyed or smoked reed.
8. Weave 3 rows ½" reed.
9. Trim and tuck stakes.
10. Weave in ends of handle.
11. Use 5/8" reed for inside and outside rims and fill with sea grass.
12. Lash with ¼" reed.

Berry Basket with Chicken Feet

Materials:
3/16" FO reed
¼" FF reed dyed or 5/8" FF reed dyed
3/8" FF reed
½" FF reed
5/8" FF reed
sea grass

Cutting:
4 fillers of 3/8" FF reed 12" long
5 stakes of 5/8" FF reed 18" long
5 stakes of 5/8" FF reed 20" long
1 handle of 5/8" FF reed 22" long

Weaving:
1. Lay the five 20" stakes horizontally with rough sides up.
2. Weave one of the 18" stakes in the center of the 20" stakes weaving under, over, under, over, under.
3. Weave two stakes on each side of the center stake. Base should be 5" x 7".
4. Weave a 3/8" filler on each side of the 2nd and 4th long stakes weaving same overs and unders.
5. Make chicken feet.
6. Bend stakes up.
7. Weave 3 rows of ½" reed.
8. Weave 3 rows of ¼" dyed or smoked reed or 1 row of 5/8" dyed reed.
9. Weave 3 rows ½" reed.
10. Trim and tuck stakes.
11. Weave in ends of handle.
12. Use 5/8" reed for inside and outside rims and fill with sea grass.
13. Lash with 3/16" FO reed.

Small Berry Basket

Materials:
3/16" FO reed
1/4" FF reed
3/8" FF reed
1/2" FF reed
5/8" FF reed
1/4" FF reed smoked
sea grass

Cutting:
Cut 3 pieces of 5/8" FF reed 17" long
Cut 5 pieces of 5/8" FF reed 13" long
Cut 1 piece of 5/8" FF reed 16" long

Weaving:
1. Lay the 3 - 5/8" stakes horizontally on the table and weave the 5 - 5/8" pieces vertically with the center stake going over-under-over. Base should be 3 1/2" x 7".
2. Bend stakes up.
3. Weave 3 rows 3/8" FF reed.
4. Weave 3 rows 1/4" FF reed smoked.
5. Weave 2 rows 3/8" FF reed.
6. Weave 1 row 1/4" FF reed for false rim.
7. Trim and tuck.
8. Insert handle.
9. Use 1/2" FF reed for inner rim and outer rim. Fill with sea grass.
10. Lash with 3/16" FO.

Basket with Ribbed Handle

Materials:
3/16" FO reed
3/8" FF reed
½" FF reed
½" FO reed
¾" FF reed
¾" FF reed, dyed
#6 round reed

Cutting:
Cut 8 stakes of 5/8" FF reed 23" long
Cut 7 stakes of 5/8" FF reed 28" long
Cut 6 fillers of ½" FF reed 17" long
Cut 1 piece of ¾" FF reed for handle 56" long
Cut 2 pieces of #6 round reed 18" long

Weaving
1. Mark centers of stakes, fillers and handle.
2. Lay the 28" stakes horizontally on the table.
3. Lay the 56" handle piece vertically on the centers.
4. Lay the filler stakes on top of the handle.
5. Weave 4 of the 23" stakes vertically on each side of the handle. Base should be 7 ½" x 12"
6. Split ends of fillers to make chicken feet.
7. Bend stakes up.
8. Weave 7 rows of 3/8" FF reed, 1 row of ¾" dyed reed, 5 rows of 3/8" FF reed.
9. Trim and tuck.
10. Push handle ends in to make handle approx. 16" long
11. Clip a piece of #6 round reed to each edge of handle and wrap with 3/16" FO reed as follows:
    a) Insert the end of the 3/16" FO reed on the right side of the handle between the handle and the round reed with the oval side against the handle.
    b) Bring the reed across the front of the handle to the left and insert it between the handle and the round reed on the left.
    c) Wrap it around the #6 reed (oval side out) and insert it between the round reed and the handle and across under the handle.
    d) Bring it up between the handle and the right side round reed, wrap around the round reed, come up and go across the top of the handle to the left.
    e) Repeat steps b – d to the other end of the handle.
12. Use ½" FO reed for out rim and ½" FF reed for inner rim. Fill #6 round reed and lash with 3/16" FO reed.

Small Things Basket #1

Materials:
3/16" FO reed
¼" FF reed
3/8" FF reed
3/8" FO reed
½" FF reed
5/8" FF reed
round reed
sea grass

Cutting:
3 stakes of ½" reed 15" long
6 stakes of 5/8" reed 11" long

Weaving:
1. Lay 3 pieces ½" reed horizontally and weave 5 pieces 5/8" reed so that the base is 2 ½" x 6".
2. Twine around the base one time with round reed.
3. Bend stakes to inside.
4. Weave 10 rows ¼" reed or other to make basket 2 ½" high.
5. Trim and tuck stakes.
6. Insert handle.
7. Use 3/8" FF reed for inner rim and 3/8" FO reed for rim and fill with sea grass.
8. Lash with 3/16" reed
9. Wrap handle with ¼" reed.

Small Things Basket #2

Materials
3/16" FO reed
3/8" FF reed
½" FF reed, dyed
5/8" FF reed
sea grass

Cut
3 stakes of 5/8" reed 17" long
4 stakes of 5/8" reed 13" long
1 handle of 5/8" reed 25" long
2 fillers of 3/8" reed 7" long

Weaving
1. Lay 3 – 17" pieces 5/8" reed horizontally.
2. Weave the handle piece under, over, under at the center of the horizontal stakes.
3. Weave 2 of the 13" pieces on each side of the handle. Pull the handle piece back so the stakes are even at the front and roll the handle into a circle and clip it with a clothespin.
4. Weave the 2 – 7" fillers between the horizontal pieces weaving them the same as the 1st and 3rd pieces.
5. Push the horizontal stakes tightly together so that base is 2 ¾" x 7".
6. Bend stakes up.
7. Weave 4 rows 3/8" reed, 1 row dyed ½" reed, and 2 rows 3/8" reed.
8. Trim and tuck stakes.
9. Insert handle end on opposite side of basket.
10. Use ½" FF reed for inner and outer rims fill with sea grass.
11. Lash with 3/16" FO reed

Sea Grass Basket #1

Materials:
1/4" FO reed
1/2" FF reed
5/8" FF reed
5/8" FO reed
3/4" FF reed
sea grass

Cutting:
Cut 5 stakes of 3/4" FF reed 18" long
Cut 5 stakes of 3/4" FF reed 20" long
Cut 4 fillers of 1/2" reed 7 1/4" long

Weaving:
1. Lay the 18" stakes vertically and weave the 20" stakes horizontally weaving the center stake under the ends and the center. Bottom should be 6" by 7 1/2".
2. Weave the fillers between the horizontal stakes.
3. Roll sides up gently so that stakes do not break.
4. With two pieces of sea grass, chase weave until there are 11 rows of woven sea grass.
5. Weave 1 row of maple strip.
6. Chase weave until there are 6 rows of sea grass.
7. Weave a false rim of 5/8" FF reed.
8. Use 3/4" FF reed for out and inner rim and fill with sea grass.
9. Cut a piece of 5/8" FO reed for handle. Cut into the oval surface 1" from each end. Shave off the oval for about 1/2" above the cuts to make a notch. Shave off the ends. Push the handle under the inner rim so that the notch catches the false rim.
10. Lash with 1/2" FO reed.

Sea Grass Basket #2

Materials:
3/16" FO reed
1/2" FF reed
5/8" FF reed
5/8" FO reed
3/4" FF reed
#2 round reed
#6 round reed.
sea grass

Cutting:
Cut 5 stakes of 5/8" FF reed 28" long
Cut 7 stakes of 5/8" FF reed 24" long

Weaving:
1. Lay the 28" stakes horizontally and weave the 24" stakes vertically so that the bottom measures 6" x 9".
2. Twine once around the bottom with #2 round reed.
3. Bend stakes up.
4. Weave 5 rows of 3/4" FF reed with 2 rows of sea grass woven together between them.
5. Weave a false rim of 1/2" FF reed.
6. Trim and tuck.
7. Use 5/8" FO reed for outer rim, 5/8" FF reed for inner rim and fill with #6 round reed.
8. Cut a piece of 5/8" FO reed for handle. Cut into the oval surface 1" from each end. Shave off the oval for about 1/2" above the cuts to make notches. Shave off the ends. Push the handle under the inner rim so that the notch catches the false rim.
9. Single or double lash with 3/16" FO reed.

Homespun Basket

Materials:
8x10 D-handle
#2 round reed
3/16" FO reed
3/8" FF reed
½" FF reed
½" FO reed
¼" FF reed, dyed
sea grass

Cutting:
7 spokes of 5/8" FF reed 29" long
6 spokes of 5/8" FF reed 26" long
6 fillers of ½" FF reed 16" long

Weaving:
1. Mark centers of spokes and fillers.
2. Lay the 29" spokes horizontally under the handle.
3. Lay the 6 filler spokes over the handle between the horizontal spokes.
4. Hold the spokes in place on one side of the handle and weave in 3 vertical spokes on the other side.
5. Weave in the other 3 vertical spokes on the opposite side.
6. Pack tightly. Base should be 8" x 10".
7. Split the fillers and tuck in "chicken feet style".
8. Twine around the base with round reed for two rows.
9. Bend stakes up.
10. Continue weaving as follows so that finished basket measures 8 x 10 x 6:
    4 rows 3/8" FF reed
    3 row 1/4" FF reed, dyed
    9 rows 3/8" FF reed
11. Trim and tuck
12. Use ½" FO for inner and outer rims and fill with sea grass.
13. Lash with 3/16" FO reed

Hearth Basket

Materials:
8" x 12" D handle
1/4" FO reed
3/8" FF reed
1/2" FF reed
5/8" FF reed
1" FF reed
#3 round reed

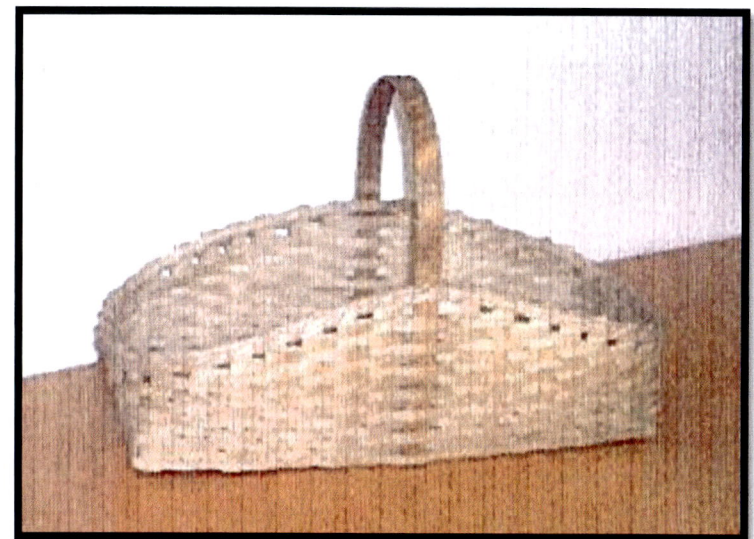

Cutting:
Cut 5 horizontal stakes of 5/8" FF reed 32" long
Cut 2 horizontal stakes of 1" FF reed 32" long
Cut 6 fillers of 3/8" FF reed 26" long
Cut 14 vertical stakes of 5/8" FF reed 24" long

Weaving:
1. Mark centers of several of each type of cut reed.
2. Lay the six 3/8" fillers horizontally on the table.
3. Place handle on the centers.
4. Lay 32" horizontal stakes on top of handle in this order: one 5/8", one 1", three 5/8", one 1", one 5/8". (Note: The 5/8" stakes are on the outside of the fillers.)
5. Weave seven 5/8" FF pieces on each side of handle so that basket bottom is 8" x 18.5".
6. Turn basket over, make chicken feet and tuck in fillers
7. Turn basket right side up and bend stakes up.
8. Weave 7 rows of 3/8" FF reed weaving first row outside handle.
9. Weave 7 rows on sides only decreasing one stake on each end of each row, tucking ends under third stake or under handle.
10. Twine 3 rows with #3 round reed.
11. Trim and tuck.
12. Make an inner rim of 1/2" FO reed.
13. Lash with 1/4" FO reed.

Hearth Basket with Wood Base

Materials:
10" x 18" wood base with 10" x 14" handle attached
#3 round reed
3/8" FF reed
½" FO reed
¾" FF reed
¼" FO reed

Cutting:
Cut 22 stakes of 5/8" FF reed 6.5" long
Cut 8 stakes each 7", 8" and 9" of 5/8" FF reed.

Weaving:
1. Insert nine 6.5" stakes evenly on each end of base. On sides, beginning at handle, insert two 9" stakes, two 8" stakes, two 7" stakes and one 6.5" stake.
2. Twine 1 row with #3 round reed.
3. Bend stakes up.
4. Weave 1 row with ¾" FF reed weaving over the handle.
5. Weave 6 rows of 3/8" FF reed.
6. Weave 7 rows on sides only decreasing one stake on each end of each row tucking ends under third stake or under handle.
7. Twine 3 rows of #3 round reed with step-ups.
8. Trim and tuck end stakes and stakes next to handle. Cut off remaining stakes to ½" and bend them at an angle so that they will be hidden under the rim.
9. Make an inner rim of ½' FO reed.
10. Lash with ¼" FO reed.

Mini Hearth Basket

Materials:
¼" FF reed
3/8" FF reed
Sea grass

Cutting:
Cut 1 pieces of 3/8" FF reed 40" long for handle stake
Cut 5 pieces of 3/8" FF reed for horizontal stakes
Cut 2 pieces each of 3/8" FF reed for vertical stakes: 17", 16", 15", 14", 13"

Weaving:
1. Lay the 5 horizontal stakes on the table approx. 3/8" apart.
2. Weave the handle stake vertical in the center going under the first horizontal stake, over the second, etc.
3. Weave the remaining stakes in descending order. Base should be 3 ½" x 8 ½".
4. Bend the stakes up.
5. Weave 4 rows with 3/8" FF reed.
6. After the 4th row, weave the sides only. Begin and end each row by weaving around the first two and last two stakes tucking ends behind the second stake. Shorten the rows by one stake at each end each time. Weave 5 rows altogether.
7. Weave a false rim row of ¼" FF reed going behind the handle on both sides and alternating overs and unders. On the ends the weaving will coincide with the last row. Push it down so the rows are completely together. Begin and end the false rim on one end of the basket.
8. Trim and tuck.
9. Insert handle ends in opposite sides and push down to base. Wrap with ¼" FF reed.
10. Using 3/8" FF reed, form inner rim wrapping around the handles. Form outer rim of 3/8" reed wrapping again around the handles.
11. Lash with ¼" FF reed.

Clammer Basket

Materials:
8x12 D handle
11/64" FO reed
¼" FF reed, dyed
3/8" FF reed
½" FF reed
5/8" FF reed
sea grass

Cutting:
Cut 13 stakes of 5/8" FF reed 28" long
Cut 6 fillers of ½" FF reed 12" long

Weaving:
1. Weave 7 of the 28" stakes over and under the base of the handle with the first and last going under.
2. Weave three 28" stakes on each side of the handle. Base should be 8" x 8".
3. Weave a filler on each side of each stake that crosses over the handle weaving same as the stake.
4. Bend the ends of the fillers even with the edge of the base and tuck under crossing stakes.
5. Bend stakes up.
6. Weave 3 rows of ½" FF reed, 3 rows of ¼" FF dyed reed, 3 rows ½" FF reed, 3 rows ¼" dyed reed, 3 rows ½" FF reed, 1 row 3/8" FF reed. Pull weavers tight so that basket tapers at the top.
    7. Use ½" FF reed for inner and outer rims, fill with sea grass and double lash with 11/64" FO reed.

Clammer Basket with Wood Base

Materials:
8"x8" wood base with 8x12 sharp
   D handle attached
11/64" FO reed
¼" FF reed, dyed
3/8" FF reed
½" FF reed
5/8" FF reed
#3 round reed
sea grass

Cutting:
Cut 26 stakes of 5/8" FF reed 10" long

Weaving:
1. Insert 3 stakes on each side of the handles and 7 stakes on the other two sides.
2. Twine 1 row with #3 round reed.
3. Bend stakes up.
4. Weave 3 rows of ½" FF reed, 3 rows of ¼" FF dyed reed, 3 rows ½" FF reed, 3 rows ¼" dyed reed, 3 rows ½" FF reed, 1 row 3/8" FF reed. Pull weavers tight so that basket tapers at the top.
5. Use ½" FF reed for inner and outer rims, fill with sea grass and double lash with 11/64" FO reed.

Utility Basket

Materials:
3/16" FO reed
½" FF reed
5/8" FF reed
¾" FF reed dyed
sea grass

Cutting:
Cut 11 stakes of 5/8" FF reed 26" long
Cut 7 stakes of 5/8" FF reed 32" long

Weaving
1. Mark centers of all cut stakes and lay the 32" stakes horizontally on the table.
2. Weave the 26" stakes vertically over and under the horizontal stakes.
3. Bend stakes up.
4. Weave 3 rows of 5/8" FF reed, 1 row of sea grass, 1 row of ¾" FF reed dyed, 1 row sea grass, 3 rows 5/8" FF reed, 1 row ½" FF reed.
5. Trim and tuck.
6. Use 5/8" FF for inner rim, 5/8" FF for outer rim, fill with sea grass and lash with 3/16" FO reed.

3 Nested Baskets

Materials:
Round wood bases — 3.5" (4.5", 5.5")
#2 round reed
3/16" FO reed
¼" FF reed
3/8" FF reed
½" FF reed
½" FF reed, dyed
½" FO reed
Sea grass

Cutting:
Small—Cut 16 spokes of ½" FF reed 6.5" long
Medium—Cut 20 spokes of ½" FF reed 7" long
Large—Cut 24 spokes of ½" FF reed 7.5" long

Weaving:
1. Insert stakes evenly around base.
2. Twine 1 row with #2 round reed.
3. Weave 11 (13, 15) rows of ¼" FF reed bring bowl to a diameter of 6" (7", 8").
4. Weave 1 row of ½" FF dyed reed.
5. Weave a false rim row of 3/8" FF reed.
6. Trim and tuck.
7. Using ½" FF reed for inner rim and ½" FO reed for outer rim, fill with sea grass and lash with 3/16" FO reed.

Chapter 2: Market Baskets

Market Basket with Wood Bottom

Materials:
7 ½"x13 ½" rectangular wood base
8" sq. oak handle
#2 round reed
3/16" FO reed
3/8" FF reed
5/8" FO reed
¼" FO reed smoked
1/2" FF reed smoked
5/8" FF reed smoked
sea grass

Cutting:
Cut 32 stakes of 5/8" FF reed 9 ½" long
Cut 32 pieces of ¼" FO reed smoked 16" long

Weaving:
1. Insert 9 stakes on long sides of base and 7 stakes on short sides.
2. Twine 1 row with #2 round reed.
3. Bend stakes up.
4. Weave 2 rows of 3/8" FF reed.
5. Weave 1 row of 5/8" FF reed smoked.
6. Twine 2 rows with #2 round reed.
7. Weave diagonally with the pieces of ¼" FO reed smoked.
8. Twine 2 rows with #2 round reed.
9. Weave 1 row of 5/8" FF reed smoked.
10. Weave 3 rows of 3/8" FF reed.
11. Use 5/8" FO reed for inner and outer rims and fill with sea grass.
12. Insert handle between rims and lash with ¼" FO reed.

Market Basket with Woven Rim

Materials:
8 x 10 D handle
3/16" FO reed
1/4" FF reed
3/8" FF reed
1/2" FF reed
3/16" FO smoked reed
5/8" FF smoked reed
#2 round reed

Cutting:
Cut 7 stakes of 1/2" FF reed 30" long
Cut 8 stakes of 1/2" FF reed 25" long
Cut 6 fillers of 5/8" FF reed 15" long
Cut 32 rim weavers of #2 round reed 28" long

Weaving:
1. Lay the 6 fillers horizontally on the table and place the handle vertically at their centers.
2. Lay the 30" stakes on top of the handle between the fillers.
3. Weave four 25" stakes on each side of handle. Bottom of basket should measure 7 ¾ "x 11".
4. Make chicken feet.
5. Weave a locking row around the base with 3/16" FO. Starting on the second stake on a long side, lay the reed on top of the stake with the oval side down. Weave to the corner and miter all corners by turning the reed over to form a 45 degree angle. End by overlapping the beginning. (Locking row is part of base.)
6. Bend stakes up.
7. Weave 6 rows with 3/8" FF reed, 1 row 3/16" FO smoked reed, 1 row 5/8" FF smoked reed, 1 row 3/16" FO smoked reed, 1 row 3/8" FF reed, 3 rows 3/16" FO reed, 6 rows ¼" FF reed. Flare the ends of the basket slightly as you weave the last few rows of ¼" FF reed.
8. Twine 3 rows with #2 round reed.
9. Make sure that the stakes are very wet, then gently trim and tuck. Try not to break them since they will not be covered.
10. Weave Gretchen border as follows:
    - Insert the #2 round pieces hairpin style between the stakes under the twining pulling them up tight against the twining.
    - Tie a string around one of the pieces of round reed.
    - Bend the tied piece and the next 2 pieces to the right of it toward the outside of the basket.
    - Bring the piece on the left over the other two, pull it down and hold it down with your left-hand fingers.
    - Add the next piece on the right to the two in your hand, bring the left piece over and down.

- Repeat the last step around the basket. When only two pieces are left, push up the piece with the string and insert the left piece into the loop formed by the stringed piece. Then push up the piece to the right of the stringed piece and push the last loop into the loop formed closer to the basket (behind two loops).
- Repeat the above steps until the twining is completely covered--about 6 rows altogether.
- Trim ends to about 1" and tuck them under the rim.

Fancy Swing-Handle Market Basket

Materials:
8" x 12" swing handle
#2 round reed
1/4" FF reed, natural and dyed
1/4" FO reed
3/8" FF reed
1/2" FF reed, natural and dyed
1/2" FO reed
5/8" FF reed
3/4" FF reed dyed
sea grass

Cutting:
Cut 7 stakes of 5/8" FF reed 32" long
Cut 8 stakes of 5/8" FF reed 26" long
Cut 6 fillers of 1/2" FF reed 18" long
Cut 32 weavers of 1/4" FO reed 16" long

Weaving:
1. Lay the six 18" fillers horizontally on the table and place the handle on their centers.
2. Lay the seven 32" stakes on top of the handle with the fillers between them.
3. Weave 4 of the 26" stakes vertically on each side of the handle to make a 7 1/2" x 13 1/2" bottom.
4. Split the ends of the fillers to make chicken feet and tuck them.
5. Twine 1 row with #2 round reed.
6. Bend stakes up.
7. Weave 2 rows of 3/8" FF reed weaving the first row outside the handle.
8. Weave 1 row of 3/4" dyed FF reed.
9. Twine 3 rows with #2 round reed.
10. Weave the 32 pieces of 1/4" FO reed diagonally.
11. Twine 3 rows with #2 round reed.
12. Weave 1 row 1/2" FF dyed reed, 3 rows 3/8" FF reed.
13. Trim and tuck.
14. Using 1/2" FO reed for inner and outer rims, fill with sea grass and single lash with 1/4" FF reed or double lash with 3/16" FO reed.
15. Wrap handle with 1/4" FF reed (11'). After wrapping around twice, lay a piece of 1/4" FF dyed reed on the handle and wrap over and under it as the handle is wrapped.

Square-Bottom Market Basket

Materials:
10"x14" D handle
3/16" FO reed
1/2" FF reed
5/8" FF reed
5/8" FO reed
1/4" FF reed dyed
#2 round reed
sea grass

Cutting:
Cut 13 pieces of 5/8" FF reed 33" long

Weaving:
1. Mark centers of cut pieces on the rough side.
2. Lay 7 of the cut pieces vertically on the table with the marked side up.
3. Weave the handle across the center marks with the first and last spoke over the handle.
4. Weave the other 6 spokes horizontally with 3 on each side of the handle. (Base--10"x10")
5. Twine once around base with #2 round reed.
6. Bend stakes up and weave 3 rows 5/8" FF reed bending corners only on the first row. Pull in slightly so that the top will be a 10" circle.
7. Weave 17 rows 1/4" FF reed dyed.
8. Weave 3 rows 5/8" FF reed and 1 row 1/2" FF reed.
9. Trim and tuck.
10. Use 5/8" FF reed for inner rim and 5/8" FO reed for outer rim. Fill with sea grass.
11. Lash with 3/16" FO reed.

Herringbone Market Basket

Materials:
12"x12" D handle
3/8" FF reed
½" FO reed
5/8" FF reed
#1 round reed
#6 round reed

Cutting:
Cut 17 pieces of 5/8" FF reed 32" long
Cut 18 pieces of 5/8" FF reed 30" long

Weaving:
1. Stand handle on flat surface and lay the 32" pieces across base with 2 pieces above handle, 2 pieces below, etc. ending with one over.
2. Weave nine 30" pieces on each side of handle. To achieve herringbone pattern, weave over 2/under 2 with each woven piece advancing one stake to stagger the weaving and form the pattern.
3. Bend all stakes up.
4. Weave 8 rows of 5/8" FF reed in herringbone pattern.
5. Weave 1 row of 3/8" FF reed for false rim.
6. Trim and tuck as follows: tuck one stake from each outside pair and trim remaining stakes even with top.
7. Use ½" FO reed for inner and outer rims, fill with #6 round reed and lash with #1 round reed.

Chapter 3: Williamsburg Baskets

Small Williamsburg Basket

Materials:
5"x9" Williamsburg handle
3/16" FO reed
1/4" FF reed
3/8" FF reed
3/8" FO reed
1/2" FF reed
1/4" FF reed dyed
#2 round reed
sea grass

Cutting:
Cut 7 pieces of ½" FF reed 24" long
Cut 10 pieces of ½" FF reed 19" long

Weaving:
1. Lay the 7 - 1/2" stakes (24") horizontally on the table and weave handle to center with first and last stakes under handle.
2. Weave 5 - 1/2" stakes (19") vertically on each side of handle. Base is 5" x 10".
3. Twine 1 round of #2 round reed.
4. Bend stakes up.
5. Weave 1 row 3/8" FF reed.
6. Weave 15 rows 1/4" FF reed.
7. Weave 3 rows 1/4" FF reed dyed.
8. Weave 1 row 1/4" FF reed for false rim.
9. Trim and tuck.
10. Use 3/8" FF reed for inner rim and 3/8" FO for outer rim. Fill with sea grass.
11. Lash with 3/16" FO.

Large Williamsburg Basket

Materials:
7 x 12 1/2 Williamsburg handle
1/4" FO reed
½" FF reed
5/8" FF reed
5/8" FO reed
1" FF reed
sea grass

Cutting:
Cut 7 pieces 5/8" FF reed 38" long
Cut 8 pieces 5/8" FF reed 30" long
Cut 2 pieces 1/2" FF reed 20" long
Cut 4 pieces 3/8" FF reed 20" long

Weaving:
1. Mark centers of base of handle and all cut pieces on rough side.
2. Lay the long stakes horizontally on the table with marked side up.
3. Weave the handle across the center marks with the first and last spokes under the handle.
4. Weave the 30" stakes vertically with half of them on each side of the handle. Base – 7" x 15".
5. Weave the two 1/2" fillers into base on inside of edge stakes weaving same as edge stakes.
6. Weave the four 3/8" fillers on both sides of the 3rd and 5th stakes weaving same as 3rd and 5th stakes.
7. Trim and tuck fillers and make chicken feet.
8. Bend the stakes up.
9. Weave 7 rows of 5/8" FF reed, 1 row of 1" FF reed, 5 rows of 1/4" FO reed, 1 row of 1" FF reed, 1 row of 1/2" FF reed.
10. Trim and tuck.
11. Use 5/8" FF reed for inner rim, 5/8" FO reed for outer rim and fill with sea grass.
12. Lash with 1/4" FO reed.

Williamsburg Twill Basket

Material:
7" Williamsburg handle
3/16" FO reed
3/8" FF reed
½" FF reed
5/8" FF reed
5/8" FO reed
#2 round reed
#2 round reed smoked
Sea grass

Cutting:
Cut 17 stakes 25" long from 1/2" FF reed. (For closed bottom make the stakes 27" long)

Weaving:
1. Lay 4 stakes horizontally and place handle across their centers.
2. Lay 5 stakes on top of handle. (For a closed bottom, go to instructions below.)
3. Weave 4 stakes on each side of handle.
4. Base should be 7 ½" x 7 ½".
5. Twine 1 row with #2 round reed.
6. Bend stakes up.
7. Weave 4 rows of 3/8" FF reed.
8. Triple twine 2 rows with ½" smoked round reed doing a step-up between rows.
9. Twill weave 14 rows of 3/16" FO reed going over 2, under 1. Move 1 stake to the right when starting each row. On the first row be sure to go over the stake before the handle and the handle.
10. Repeat step 8.
11. Weave 5 rows of 3/8" FF reed.
12. Trim and tuck.
13. Use 5/8" FF reed for inner rim, 5/8" FO reed for outer rim and fill with sea grass or fiber rush.
14. Lash with 3/16" FO reed.

Alternate instructions for closed bottom:
- Add 8 fillers 12" long to cutting list.
- Weave one stake on each side of handle. Weave a filler on both sides of the stakes that go under the handle weaving same as the stakes. Weave remaining vertical stakes treating the stakes and fillers that go under the handle as one stake. Base should be 7 ½" x 8 ½".
- Make chicken feet.
- Continue with step 5 above.

Williamsburg Tote with Color

Materials:
7" Williamsburg handle
¼" FO reed
3/8" FF reed
½" FF reed
½" FF reed dyed
5/8" FF reed
5/8" FO reed
sea grass

Cutting:
Cut 17 spokes of 5/8" FF reed 24" long
Cut 6 fillers of 3/8" FF reed 13" long

Weaving:
1. Lay 7 spokes horizontally and place handle across their centers.
2. Lay the 6 fillers on top of handle.
3. Weave 3 spokes on each side of handle.
4. Base should be 7 ½" x 7 ½".
5. Make chicken feet.
6. Weave 11 rows 3/8" FF reed, 3 rows 1/2" FF reed dyed, 1 row ½" reed.
    Be sure to watch the shape of the basket as you weave. The non-handle sides must have the same shape as the handle sides so they must be flared. An easy way to do this is to leave a slight gap between stakes when rounding the corners. Measure often to make sure that the width across the basket is the same as the width between the handles. The top of the basket should be a circle with a height of 6".
7. Trim and tuck.
8. Use 5/8" FF reed for inner rim, 5/8" FO reed for outer rim and fill with sea grass.
9. Lash with ¼" FO reed.

Square-Bottom Williamsburg Basket - Small

Materials:
5" Williamsburg handle
3/16" FO reed
¼" FF reed
3/8" FF reed
3/8" FO reed
#2 round reed
sea grass

Cutting:
Cut 13 spokes of 3/8" FF reed 19" long

Weaving:
1. Lay 3 spokes horizontally and place handle across their centers.
2. Lay 4 spokes on top of handle.
3. Weave 3 spokes on each side of handle.
4. Base should be 5" x 5".
5. Bend stakes up.
6. Weave 12 rows ¼" FF reed, 2 rows #2 round reed, 1 row ½" FF reed, 2 rows #2 round reed, 2 rows ¼" FF reed. Be sure to watch the shape of the basket as you are weaving. The non-handle sides should have the same shape as the handle sides so they must be flared. An easy way to do this is to leave a slight gap when rounding the corners. Measure frequently to make sure that the width across the basket is the same as the width between the handles. The basket should be a circle at the top. (You may change the pattern if you wish. Just be sure to end with a row of ¼" FF reed and a height of approx. 5".)
7. Trim and tuck.
8. Use 3/8" FF reed for inner rim, 3/8" FO reed for outer rim and fill with sea grass.
9. Lash with 3/16" FO reed.

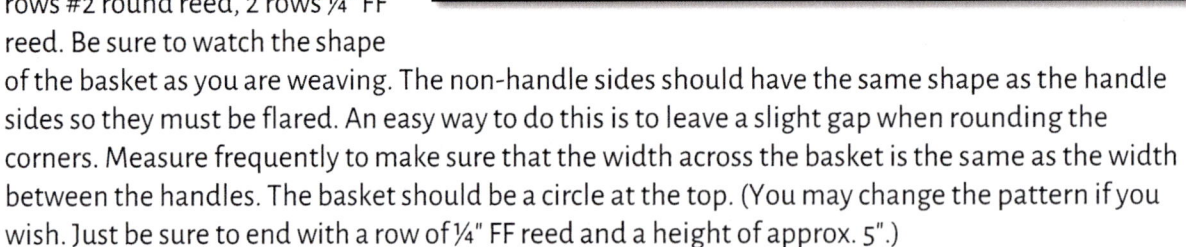

Square-Bottom Williamsburg Basket - Medium

Materials:
7" Williamsburg handle
3/16" FO reed
3/8" FF reed
½" FF reed
½" FO reed
5/8" FF reed
sea grass

Cutting:
Cut 17 spokes of ½" FF reed 28" long

Weaving:
1. Lay 4 spokes horizontally and place handle across their centers.
2. Lay 5 spokes on top of handle.
3. Weave 4 spokes on each side of handle.
4. Base should be 7 ½" x 7 ½".
5. Bend stakes up.
6. Weave 10 rows 3/8" FF reed, 1 row 5/8" FF reed, 3 rows 3/16" FO reed, 1 row 5/8" FF reed, 3 rows 3/8" FF reed. Be sure to watch the shape of the basket as you weave. The non-handle sides must have the same shape as the handle sides so they must be flared. An easy way to do this is to leave a slight gap between stakes when rounding the corners. Measure often to make sure that the width across the basket is the same as the width between the handles. The top of the basket should be a circle with a height of 7-7½".
7. Trim and tuck.
8. Use 1/2" FF reed for inner rim, 1/2" FO reed for outer rim and fill with sea grass or fiber rush.
9. Lash with 3/16" FO reed.

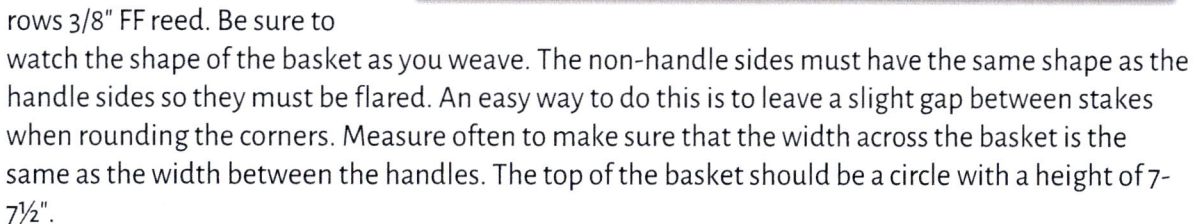

Square-Bottom Williamsburg Basket – Large

Materials:
10" Williamsburg handle
3/16" FO reed
3/8" FF reed
½" FF reed
½" FO reed
5/8" FF reed
7/8" FF reed
sea grass

Cutting:
Cut 17 spokes of 5/8" FF reed 30" long

Weaving:
1. Lay 4 spokes horizontally and place handle across their centers.
2. Lay 5 spokes on top of handle.
3. Weave 4 spokes on each side of handle.
4. Base should be 10 x 10.
5. Bend stakes up.
6. Weave 10 rows ½" FF reed, 2 rows ¼" FO reed, 1 row 7/8" FF reed, 2 rows ¼" FO reed, 1 row ½" FF reed, 1 row 3/8" FF reed. Be sure to watch the shape of the basket as you are weaving. The non-handle sides should have the same shape as the handle sides so they must be flared. An easy way to do this is to leave a slight gap when rounding the corners. Measure frequently to make sure that the width across the basket is the same as the width between the handles. The basket should be a circle at the top. (You may change the pattern if you wish. Just be sure to end with a row of 3/8" FF reed and a height of approx. 8".)
7. Trim and tuck.
8. Use ½" FF reed for inner rim, ½" FO reed for outer rim and fill with sea grass.
9. Lash with 3/16" FO reed.

Chapter 4: Baskets for Around the House

Stair Basket

Materials:
10 x 20 D handle
#2 round reed
¼" FF or FO reed dyed
3/16" FO reed
½" FF reed
5/8" FF reed
5/8" FO reed
seagrass

Cutting:
Cut 7 pieces of 5/8" FF reed 50" long
Cut 6 pieces of 5/8" FF reed 42" long
Cut 7 pieces of 5/8" FF reed 26" long

Weaving:
1. Mark center of base of handle and mark centers of all cut pieces on rough side.
2. Lay the 50" pieces vertically on the table with marked side up.
3. Weave the handle across the center marks with the first and last spoke over the handle.
4. Weave 5 of the 42" spokes below the handle and the remaining 42" spoke above the handle. (Base should be 9 ½" wide and 8 ½" long)
5. Twine two rows around the base with #2 round reed.
6. Bend the stakes up and using 5/8" FF reed weave one row weaving outside the handle.
7. Continue weaving with 5/8" FF reed weaving 13 rows altogether.
8. With the handle end of the basket facing you, weave the 26" spokes into the 50" vertical spokes. (The new section should be 9 ½" wide and 8" high.)
9. Bend the new section down 90 degrees and twine 2 rows with #2 round reed.
10. Bend the spokes up in the new section and weave two rows of 5/8" FF reed around the entire basket.
11. Weave 5 rows ¼" dyed reed, 2 rows 5/8" FF reed, and 1 row ½" FF reed.
12. Trim and tuck.
13. Use 5/8" FF for inner rim and 5/8" FO for outer rim. Fill with sea grass.
14. Lash with 3/16" FO reed.

Napkin Basket

Materials:
6" square wood base
#2 round reed
¼" FF reed
3/16" FO reed
3/8" FF reed
½" FF reed
½" FO reed
5/8" FF reed
¼" FF reed dyed
½" FF reed dyed
sea grass

Cutting:
Cut 22 spokes of ½" FF reed 6 ½" long
Cut 2 spokes of 5/8" FF reed 18" long
Cut 1 piece of ½" FF reed dyed for bow 19" long
Cut 1 piece of ¼" FF reed dyed for handle 13" long
Cut 1 piece of ½" FF reed dyed 3" long
Cut 1 piece of ¼" FF to wrap handle 7' long
Cut 1 piece of 3/16" FO reed for lashing 65" long

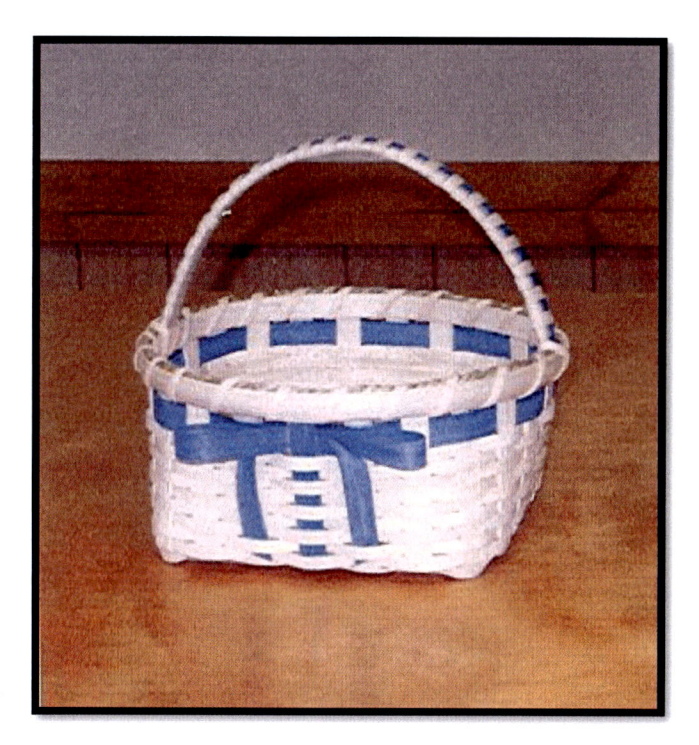

Weaving:
1. Insert five ½" FF spokes on opposite sides of base and one in each corner. Place the 5/8" spokes at centers of remaining opp sides with two ½" spokes on each side.
2. Twine, chase weave or continuous weave around the base with round reed making sure that the first row is under the corner stakes and having a total of 4 rows when finished.
3. Weave 1 row ¼" FF reed keeping stakes flat.
4. Bend stakes up and weave 9 additional rows ¼" FF reed.
5. Weave 1 row ½" FF reed dyed.
6. Insert the 3" piece of ½" FF reed on the center stake of the non-handle side.
7. Weave 1 row 3/8" FF reed for false rim.
8. Trim and tuck.
9. Use ½" FF reed for inner rim and ½" FO reed for outer rim. Fill with sea grass.
10. Insert handle ends into opposite sides between the rims.
11. Lash with 3/16" FO reed.
12. Make bow—Insert the 19" piece ½" FF reed dyed behind spoke where dyed reed was inserted with the rough side out. With the left end, make a loop to the right and being end back behind the same spoke. Do the same with the right end. Cut ends off at an angle and insert under next to bottom row of weaving.
13. Wrap handle with ¼" FF wrapping over and under a piece of ¼" FF reed dyed.

Lattice Candle Basket

Materials:
4" round wood base
3/16" FO reed
1/4" FO reed
3/8" FF reed
1/2" FF reed
1/2" FO reed
1/4" FF smoked or dyed reed
#2 round reed

Cutting:
Cut 12 stakes of ½" FF reed 8 ½" long
Cut 6 pieces of ¼" smoked or dyed reed 20" long

Weaving:
1. Insert the 12 stakes in base.
2. Chase weave 3 rows with round reed.
3. Bend stakes up and weave 2 rows 1/4" FO reed.
4. Leave 3/4" space and weave 2 more rows 1/4" FO reed.
5. Repeat above step until there are 5 pairs of FO rounds.
6. Weave a false rim of 3/8" FF reed.
7. Trim and tuck.
8. Wrap every other stake with smoked/dyed reed as follows:
   - Push a piece of 1/4" smoked reed into one of the openings above the bottom row of FO reed and out the next opening going around a stake that has the FO reed behind it on the second row.
   - Place the center of the piece of smoked reed behind the stake and bring the right end across the front of the stake.
   - Push this end of the piece into the next opening above on the left of the stake, go behind the stake and come out the opening on the right.
   - Continue winding around the stake in this manner to the top.
   - Repeat with the left end of the piece going in the opposite direction.
   - Trim all end even with top of false rim.
9. Use 1/2" FF reed for inside rim, 1/2" FO reed for outside rim, fill with sea grass and lash with 3/16" FO reed.

Tissue Box Basket #1

Materials:
Tissue box base
3/16" FO reed
1/4" FF reed
3/8" FF reed
1/2" FF reed
#2 round reed
sea grass

Cutting:
Cut 24 pieces of 1/2" FF reed 8" long

Weaving:
1. Insert the 24 cut pieces into the base with five on each side and one in each corner.
2. Weave 10 rows of #2 round reed.
3. Bend stakes up.
4. Weave 5 rows of 3/8" FF reed.
5. Weave 6 rows round reed.
6. Weave 5 rows 3/8" FF reed.
7. Weave 1 row 1/4" FF reed for false rim.
8. Trim and tuck.
9. Use 3/8" FF reed for both inner and outer rims. Fill with sea grass.
10. Lash with 3/16" FO reed.

Tissue Box Basket #2

Materials:
5" x 9.5" wood base with slot
#2 round reed
3/16" FO reed
¼" FF reed
½" FF reed
5/8" FF reed
Sea grass

Cutting:
Cut 28 stakes of 5/8" FF reed 6.5" long

Weaving:
1. Lay base on table upside-down, insert stakes with smooth sides down. Glue stakes in place.
2. Twine 2 rows with #2 round reed.
3. Bend stakes up.
4. Weave 4 rows ¼" FF reed.
5. Twine 2 rows w/#2 round reed
6. Weave 1 row 5/8" FF reed.
7. Twine 2 rows w/#2 round reed.
8. Weave 5 rows ¼" FF reed.
9. Trim and tuck.
10. Use ½" FF reed for inner and outer rims, fill with sea grass and lash with 3/16" FO reed.

Cd Holder Basket

Materials:
5" x 12" wood base
#2 round reed
3/16" FO reed
¼" FF reed
3/8" FF reed
3/8" FO reed
½" FF reed
3/16" FO reed, smoked
5/8" FF reed
rush for filler

Cutting:
Cut 36 stakes ½" FF reed 8" long
Cut 4 stakes ¼" FF reed 8" long

Weaving:
1. Insert the 36 – ½" stakes around the base having five on each end and thirteen on each side. Insert a ¼" stake in each corner.
2. Chase weave once around with #2 round reed.
3. Bend stakes up.
4. Weave one row of 3/8" FF reed, 10 rows of ¼" FF reed, 1 row 3/16" FO reed smoked, 1 row 5/8" FF reed, 1 row 3/16" FO reed smoked, 3 rows ¼" FF reed.
5. Trim and tuck.
6. Use 3/8" FF reed for inner rim and 3/8" FO reed for outer rim. Fill with rush.
7. Lash with 3/16" FO reed.

Classy Trash Basket #1

Materials:
7" x 9" wood bottom with or without 1 ½" ball feet attached
#2 round reed
3/16" FO reed
¼" FO reed
3/8" FF reed
5/8" FF reed
5/8" FO reed
3/16" FO reed, smoked
fiber rush for filler

Cutting:
Cut 28 stakes of 5/8" FF reed 15" long

Weaving:

1. Insert 1 stake in each corner, 7 stakes on each long side and 5 stakes on each short side.
2. Chase weave 3 rows with #2 round reed.
3. Weave 1 row with 3/16" FO reed lifting stakes to a 45-degree angle.
4. Weave 3 rows of 3/8" FF reed bring stakes almost straight up. The stakes should flare very slightly so that the basket is 4" - 5" larger at the top than at the bottom.
5. After the first 3 rows of weaving, lay pieces of 3/16" smoked FF reed on top of the first, second and third stakes on the front and back of the basket. Push them down so that the ends are hidden behind either the 3/16" FO row or the first 3/8" FF row.
6. Continue weaving with 3/8" FF reed until there are 18 rows altogether.
7. Weave 5 rows of 5/8" FF reed overlaying each row with 3/16" FO smoked reed.
8. Weave 3 rows of 3/8" FF reed.
9. Trim and tuck.
10. Use 5/8" FF reed for inner rim, 5/8" FO reed for outer rim and fill with fiber rush.
11. Lash with ¼" FO reed.

Classy Trash Basket #2

Materials:
7" x 9" wood bottom
#2 round reed
3/16" FO reed
¼" FO reed
3/8" FF reed
5/8" FF reed
5/8" FO reed
3/16" FO reed, smoked
fiber rush for filler

Cutting:
Cut 28 stakes of 5/8" FF reed 15" long

Weaving:
1. Insert 1 stake in each corner, 7 stakes on each long side and 5 stakes on each short side.
2. Chase weave 3 rows with #2 round reed weaving under the corner stakes on the first row.
3. Weave 2 rows with 3/16" FO reed lifting stakes to a 45 degree angle.
4. Weave 17 rows of 3/8" FF reed bring stakes up at a slight angle. The stakes should flare very slightly so that the basket is 4" - 5" larger at the top than at the bottom.
5. Weave 7 continuous rows of ½" FF smoked reed doing an over 2 under 1 twill pattern.
6. Weave 6 rows of 3/8" FF reed.
7. Trim and tuck.
8. Use 5/8" FF reed for inner rim, 5/8" FO reed for outer rim and fill with fiber rush.
9. Lash with ¼" FO reed.

Pincushion Basket

Materials:
#2 round reed
#4 round reed
3/16" FO reed, smoked or dyed
10" circle of fabric
fiberfill

Cutting:
Cut 6 pieces of #4 round reed 18" long

Weaving:
1. Lay 3 pieces of #4 round reed side-by-side horizontally on the table.
2. Lay the other 3 pieces on top of them and perpendicular to them.
3. Wrap these together by laying a piece of #2 round reed across the vertical pieces, then go down and under the horizontal pieces on the right side, come up and cross the verticals and then go under the horizontals on the left side. This is called "tying in the slath". Tie in the slath for 3 rows.
4. Separate the three vertical spokes at the top and bring the reed up between spokes 1 and 2.
5. Mark spoke 1.
6. Add another piece of #2 reed between spokes 2 and 3 and twine 6 rows around the individual spokes keeping the twining very tight.
7. Push the spokes away from you and continue twining the sides for 6 rows allowing the sides to flare slightly.
8. Rand two rows with 3/16" FO reed.
9. Twine 4 more rows with #2 round reed cutting the weavers off behind spokes 1 and 2.
10. Pinch the spokes and weave border as follows:
    - Behind one and out.
    - Over two and in.
11. Trim ends.
12. Turn basket over and push the bottom in.
13. Sew a row of running stitches around the circle of fabric, fill it with fiberfill, close the circle and place it in the basket.

Plastic Bag Basket

Materials:
Plastic bag basket base
1 bushel handle
#2 round reed
3/16" FO reed
3/8" FF reed
½" FF reed
½" FO reed
½" FF reed smoked
5/8" FF reed
sea grass

Cutting:
Cut 23 - 10" stakes of 5/8" FF reed

Weaving:
1. Insert one stake at the center of one end of base. Insert one stake on each side of the center of the other end of base. Distribute the remaining stakes evenly around the base.
2. Twine once around the base with #2 round reed.
3. Bend stakes up.
4. Trim the last 4" of smoked reed at an angle and begin weaving between the two stakes on the divided end of the base. Weaving continuously, weave a twill pattern of over 2, under 1 for 14 rows. (Approx. 7 ½" high.) Trim the last 4" at an angle and end with this angle above the angle at the beginning.
5. Weave one row of 3/8" FF reed in twill pattern for false rim.
6. Trim and tuck.
7. Push bushel handle tips into weaving on back of basket.
8. Using ½" FF reed for inner rim and ½" FO reed for outer rim, fill with sea grass and lash with 3/16" FO reed.

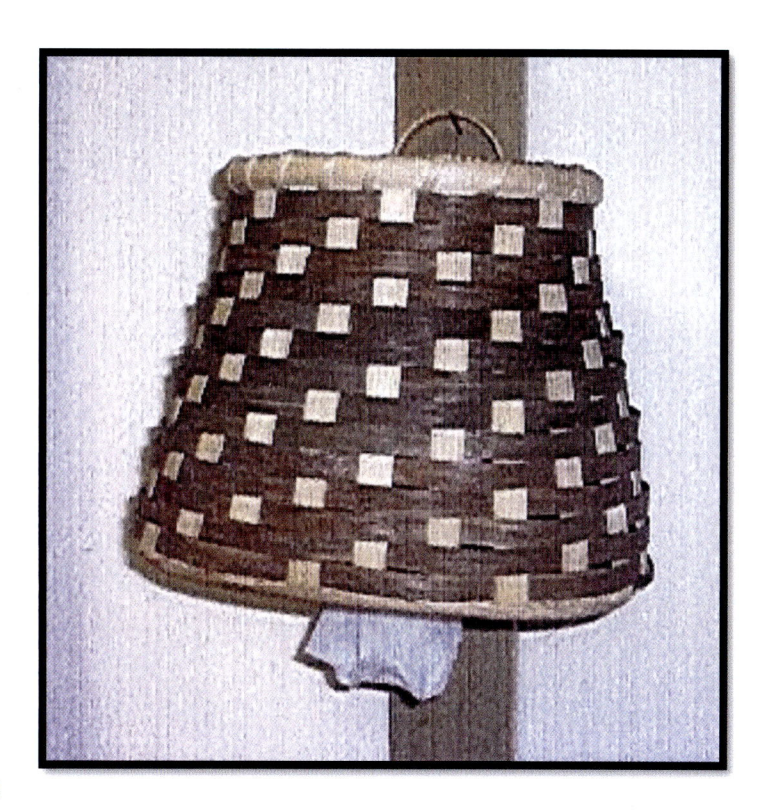

Lamp Basket

Materials:
4 ½" wood base with 1 ½" hole in center
#2 round reed
3/16" FO reed
¼" FF reed
3/8" FF reed
½" FF reed
½" FO reed
1" ash strip
4" round handle
sea grass

Cutting:
Cut 16 stakes of ½" FF reed 9" long

Weaving:
1. Insert stakes evenly in base.
2. Twine once around base with #2 round reed.
3. Bend stakes up.
4. Weave 8 rows of ¼" FF reed flaring to a diameter of 5 ½".
5. Triple weave 2 rows with #2 round.
6. Weave 1 row of 1" ash strip.
7. Triple weave 2 rows with #2 round reed.
8. Weave 10 rows of ¼" FF reed pulling in to a diameter of 4 ½".
9. Weave 1 false rim row of 3/8" FF making a diameter of 4 ¼".
10. Cut inside stakes just below top edge of false rim. Bend outside stakes to inside and trim to ½".
11. Clothespin ½" FF inner rim in place to hold cut ends of stakes down.
12. Push handle down between inside rim and false rim.
13. Add the ½" FO outside rim and a piece of sea grass on each side of handle and double lash with 3/16" FO reed.

Bathroom Tissue Basket

Materials:
5" x 14" rectangular wood base
#3 round reed
#10 round reed
¼" FO reed
½" FF reed
5/8" FF reed
5/8" FF reed dyed
5/8" FO reed
Sea grass

Cutting:
Cut 32 stakes of 5/8" FF reed 15" long
Cut 4 pieces of 5/8" FO reed 12" long
Cut 2 pieces #10 round reed 12" long

Weaving:
1. Insert one stake in each corner of the base, eleven stakes in each long side and 3 stakes in each end.
2. Twine 1 row with #3 round reed.
3. Bend stakes up.
4. Weave 5 rows of ½" FF reed weaving the first row over the corner stakes. After the 4th row, insert the four pieces of 5/8" FO reed over the four corner stakes. Clip these together and weave as one stake.
5. Weave 1 row 5/8" FF reed dyed.
6. Weave 5 rows of ½" FF reed and 1 row of 5/8" FF reed dyed 2 more times (15 rows altogether).
7. Weave 6 rows of ½" FF reed.
8. Trim and tuck.
9. Insert a handle* on each short side.
10. Use 5/8" FF reed for both inner and out rim, fill with sea grass and lash with ¼" FO reed.

To make handle:
1. Mark the 12" pieces of #10 round reed 1 ½" from each end, 2 7/8" from each end and 3 ½" from each end.
2. Soak the pieces at least 5 minutes in hot water.
3. Bend the pieces into a U shape.
4. With a knife, taper the 1 ½" ends so that they are flat at the tip.
5. Cut halfway through at the 3 ½" marks and the 2 7/8" marks. Carve out the wood between the cuts to form a notch for the rim.

Pencil Mug

Materials:
3" round wood base
3/16" FO reed
¼" FF reed
¼" FF reed, dyed red
3/8" FF reed
½" FF reed
½" FF reed, dyed blue
3/8" FO reed
Sea grass

Cutting:
Cut 11 stakes of ½" FF reed 7 ½" long.
Cut 1 handle stake of ½" FF reed 20" long

Weaving:
1. Insert the 11 stakes and the handle stake evenly in base.
2. Twine 3 rows with #2 round reed.
3. Weave 5 rows of ¼" FF reed weaving
   1st row outside handle stake, 1 row sea grass, 1 row red ¼" FF reed, 1 row navy ½" reed, 1 row red ¼" reed, 6 rows ¼" FF reed.
4. Bend handle stake back and bring end under the 1st and 3rd rows of ¼" FF reed and up under the handle to make it double. Adjust to desired length. Wrap handle with ¼" FF reed.
5. Trim and tuck.
6. Use 3/8" FF reed for inner rim, 3/8" FO for outer rim and sea grass for filler.
7. Double lash with 3/16" FO reed.

Sewing Basket

Materials:
10" round wood base (1/2" thick)
#2 round reed
#3 round reed
#4 round reed
¼" FO reed
½" FF reed
7/8" FF reed
10" square notched handle
10" scrollwork lid
Fabric

Cutting:
Cut 12 stakes of ½" FF reed 9" long
Cut 12 stakes of 7/8" FF reed 9" long
Cut 24 pieces of #3 round reed 40" long
Cut 4 pieces of #4 round reed 42" long

Weaving:
1. Insert the 24 stakes evenly in the base alternating the ½" and the 7/8" stakes. Glue in place.
2. Turn the base upside down and with 4 pieces of #4 round reed, work a 4-rod locked coil:
    a) Insert a #4 round reed weaver behind spoke #1 and the next 3 spokes.
    b) Bring the left spoke in front of three spokes, behind one and out. Continue to spoke #1.
    c) Work a step-up--bring the right weaver in front of 3 spokes and behind one. Lift the original weaver and go under it and out to lock the coil. Repeat with 3, 2 and 1.
    d) Tighten by pulling ends in opposite directions. Cut ends with a slant so that they lie flush against the other weavers.
3. Bend stakes up.
4. With #3 round reed, triple weave 4 rows with step-ups.
5. Weave 7 rows with ¼" FO weaving the first row over the ½" stakes.
6. Insert 1" spacers (for fabric).
7. Weave 4 rows of ¼" FO reed. Be sure to weave the first row the same as the last row before the spacers.
8. Weave 1 row of ½" FF reed.
9. Twine 3 rows of #3 round reed.
10. Trim and tuck spokes.
11. Work a rewoven braided border:
    a) Insert the 40" pieces of well-soaked #3 round reed under the 3 rows of twining.
    b) Form scallops by inserting ends of pieces under twining of the 2nd spoke to the right.
    c) Start with any pair of round reed pieces and take them behind the pair to the right and out.

    d) Take a pair and go under only the pair to the right and up so that you don't go inside. Do this very loosely or the next row will be too tight.
    e) Each pair must now trace the path of the pair to the right. First, it will go down to the outside
    f) and then to the inside. The braid should stand up straight and not lean in.

12. Insert handle.
13. The #3 round reed pairs on the inside will form spokes to make a lip for the basket. Using #2 round reed, twine 3 rows keeping spokes parallel to the base.
14. Use remaining length of spokes to make a simple braided border:
    a) Take a pair of spokes, go under 2 pairs to the right and up.
    b) Take a pair of spokes, go over two and to the inside.
15. Stain basket and then weave fabric into the opening created by the spacers.

Gift Wrap Basket

Materials:
5" x 14" rectangular wood base
2 small bushel handles
#2 round reed
#3 round reed, dyed dark brown
¼" FO reed
½" FF reed
5/8" FF reed
5/8" FO reed
1" FF reed
Sea grass

Cutting:
Cut 32 stakes of 5/8" FF reed 21" long
Cut 4 pieces of 5/8" FO reed 18" long

Weaving:
1. Insert one stake in each corner of the base, eleven stakes in each long side and 3 stakes in each end.
2. Twine 2 rows with #2 round reed.
3. Bend stakes up.
4. Weave 7 rows of ½" FF reed weaving the first row over the corner stakes. After weaving 4 rows, insert the four pieces of 5/8" FO reed over the four corner stakes. Clip these together and weave as one stake.
5. Twine 1 row with #3 round reed dyed, weave 1 row of 1" FF reed, twine 1 row of #3 round reed dyed.
6. Weave 13 rows of ½" FF reed.
7. Repeat step 5.
8. Weave 8 rows of ½" FF reed.
9. Trim and tuck.
10. Insert a bushel handle on each short side.
11. Use 5/8" FF reed for both inner and out rim, fill with sea grass and lash with ¼" FO reed.

Chapter 5:
Plant Baskets

Plant Basket #1

Materials:
Wood plant stand base
#2 round reed
¼" FF reed
¼" FO reed smoked
3/8" FF reed
5/8" FF reed
5/8" FO reed
sea grass

Cutting:
Cut 28 spokes of 5/8" FF reed 11" long

Weaving:
1. Insert spokes into groove of base, smooth side down.
2. Chase weave with 2 strands of #2 round reed for about ½" keeping spokes flat.
3. Bend spokes up gently and continue to weave until just past the curve—approx 16 rows of round reed.
4. Spokes should be almost upright.
5. Weave 21 rows alternating 3/8" FF reed and ¼" FO smoked reed, beginning and ending with 3/8" FF, and flaring slightly to a diameter of 10". Add one row of 3/8" FF for false rim. Basket should be 8 - 8 ½" high.
6. Trim and tuck.
7. Use 5/8" FF for inside rim and 5/8" FO for outside rim.
8. Fill with sea grass and lash with ¼" FF reed.

Plant Basket #2

Materials:
Wood plant stand base
#2 round reed
3/16" FO reed
¼" FO reed
¼" FO reed smoked
1/2" FF reed
5/8" FF reed
5/8" FO reed
sea grass

Cutting:
Cut 28 spokes of 5/8" FF reed 11" long

Weaving:
1. Insert spokes into groove of base, smooth side down.
2. Twine 2 rows of #2 round reed.
3. Weave 4 rows of 3/16" FO reed bringing stakes to almost a vertical position by the last row.
4. Weave 21 rows alternating 1/2" FF reed and 1/4" FO smoked reed, beginning and ending with 1/2" FF, and flaring slightly to a diameter of 9-10". Basket should be 8 - 8 ½" high.
5. Weave I additional row 1/2" FF for false rim.
6. Trim and tuck.
7. Use 5/8" FF for inside rim and 5/8" FO for outside rim.
8. Fill with sea grass and lash with ¼" FO reed.

Small Planter Basket #1

Materials:
4" round wood base
#2 round reed
1/4" FO reed
3/8" FF reed
1/2" FF reed

Cutting:
Cut 16 stakes of 1/2" FF reed 8" long
Cut 16 weavers of 1/4" FO reed 12" long
Cut 16 pieces of #2 round reed 22" long

Weaving:
1. Insert the 16 stakes into the base.
2. Chase weave 4 rounds with #2 round reed.
3. Bend stakes up.
4. Weave 2 rows of 3/8" FF reed.
5. Twine 3 rows with #2 round reed.
6. Weave the 1/4" FO pieces diagonally.
7. Twine 3 rows of #2 round reed.
8. Trim and tuck.

Braided edge:
1. Soak the 16 pieces of #2 round reed well and insert each one hairpin style under the upper twining going over two stakes each time to form a scalloped edge.
2. Lift two adjacent pairs of ends of round reed, bring the left one around the right one and down to the outside. Continue around basket in the same manner inserting the ends of the last pair through the loop formed by the first pair.
3. Insert one pair through the top of the next loop on the right toward the inside of the basket inserting the last pair through the first loop.
4. Repeat the last two steps to complete two rows of braiding.
5. Tuck ends under the 1/2" FF reed which was tucked previously.

Small Planter Basket #2

Materials:
4 ½" round wood base
#2 round reed
1/4" FO reed
1/2" FF reed

Cutting:
Cut 16 stakes of 1/2" FF reed 8" long
Cut 16 weavers of 1/4" FO reed 12" long
Cut 16 pieces of #2 round reed 22" long

Weaving:
1. Insert the 16 stakes into the base.
2. Twine 2 rows with #2 round reed.
3. Bend stakes up.
4. Weave 2 rows of ½" FF reed.
5. Twine 3 rows with #2 round reed.
6. Weave the 1/4" FO pieces diagonally.
7. Twine 3 rows of #2 round reed.
8. Trim and tuck.

Braided edge:
1. Soak the 16 pieces of #2 round reed well and insert each one hairpin style under the upper twining going over the second stake each time to form a scalloped edge.
2. Hold two adjacent pairs of ends of round reed, bring the left one around the right one and down to the outside. Continue around basket in the same manner inserting the ends of the last pair through the loop formed by the first pair.
3. Insert one pair through the top of the next loop on the right toward the inside of the basket inserting the last pair through the first loop.
4. Repeat the last two steps to complete two rows of braiding.
5. Tuck ends under the 1/2" FF reed which was tucked previously.

Medium Planter Basket

This basket will hold a 5" pot with a 4" saucer.

Materials:
4 ½" round wood base
#2 round reed
3/16" FO reed
½" FF reed

Cutting:
Cut 20 stakes of ½" FF reed 9" long
Cut 40 pieces of 3/16" FO reed 8 ½" long
Cut 20 pieces of #2 round reed 22" long

Weaving:
1. Insert the 20 stakes evenly around the base.
2. Chase weave 3 rows with #2 round reed. DO NOT CUT.
3. Bend stakes up.
4. Add a third strand of #2 round reed and triple weave five rows.
5. Diagonal weave around the basket with 20 of the 3/16" FO pieces.
6. Diagonal weave around again going the other direction with the other 20 FO pieces.
7. Triple weave three rows with #2 round reed.
8. Weave two rows with ½" FF reed.
9. Triple weave three rows with #2 round reed.
10. Trim and tuck all stakes inserting them under three rows of triple weave below the ½" FF reed.
11. Soak the cut pieces of #2 round reed well.
12. Insert a piece of round reed hairpin style with one end under the triple weave on any stake, skip one stake, and place the other end under the triple weave on the next stake after the skipped one. Pull the ends up to make them even and form a scallop at the bottom edge of the top row of ½" FF reed.
13. Repeat the above step around the top of the basket with all 20 pieces of round reed.
14. Weave braid as follows:
- Grasp one pair of round reed, bring it behind the pair to the right and down to the outside of the basket. Repeat this around the basket inserting the the last pair through the first loop formed.
- Insert one pair into the top of the loop on the right and push down to the inside. The last pair will be inserted into the first loop formed.
- Repeat the above two steps to complete the braided edge.
1. Trim the ends of the round reed and insert them under the tucked stakes.

Basket Vase

The shorter version of the vase will hold a pint jar and the taller version will hold a quart jar.

Materials:
4" wood base
#2 round reed
3/16" FO reed, natural and smoked
1/4" FF reed
3/8" FF reed
1/2" FF reed
1/2" FO reed
sea grass

Cutting:
Cut 20 stakes of 3/8" FF reed 10" long

Weaving:
1. Insert the 20 stakes into the base.
2. Weave 4 rounds with #2 round reed.
3. Bend stakes up and weave one round with 1/4" FF reed.
4. Weave one row with 3/8" FF reed. Weave a row of 3/16" smoked reed on top of the 3/8" reed.
5. Repeat step 4 until there are 13 rows of smoked reed for the short version or 15 rows for the taller version.
6. Weave one row of 3/8" FF reed for the false rim.
7. Use 1/2" FF reed for the inner rim, 1/2" FO reed for the outer rim and fill with sea grass.
8. Lash with 3/16" FO reed.

Round Flower Basket

Materials:
6" round wood base
#2 round reed
3/16" FO reed
¼" FF reed
3/8" FF reed
3/8" FO reed
5/8" FF reed
sea grass

Cutting:
Cut 18 pieces of 5/8" FF reed 6" long

Weaving:
1. Insert the 18 stakes evenly around the base.
2. Continuous weave 16 rows of #2 round reed. Begin lifting after the 2nd row.
3. Weave 4 rows ¼" FF reed lifting stakes until diameter is 8".
4. Weave 3 rows 3/8" FF reed.
5. Weave 1 row ¼" FF reed.
6. Using 3/8" FF reed for inner rim and 3/8" FO reed for outer rim. Fill with sea grass.
7. Lash with 3/16" FO reed.

Chapter 6: Food Baskets

Pie Basket #1

Materials:
Pie basket wood base and handle
#3 round reed
3/16" FO reed
¼" FO reed
¼" FF reed dyed
3/8" FF reed
½" FF reed
½" FO reed
¾" FF reed
Sea grass

Cutting:
Cut 22 stakes of ¾" FF reed 8" long

Weaving:
1. Insert the 22 stakes evenly around the base.
2. Chase weave the #3 round reed just past curve of handle (30 rs?).
3. Weave 1 row ¼" FO reed.
4. Weave 1 row ¼" FF reed dyed.
5. Weave 1 row ¾" FF reed.
6. Weave 1 row ¼" FF reed dyed.
7. Weave 1 row ¼" FO reed.
8. Weave 1 row 3/8" FF reed.
9. Trim and tuck.
10. Use ½" FF reed for inside rim and ½" FO reed for outside rim.
11. Fill with sea grass and lash with 3/16" FO reed.

Pie Basket #2

Materials:
Pie basket wood base and handle
#3 round reed
¼" FF reed dyed
3/8" FF reed
¾" FF reed

Cutting:
Cut 22 stakes of ¾" FF reed 8" long
Cut 24 pieces of #3 round reed 40" long

Weaving:
1. Insert the 22 stakes evenly around the base.
2. Chase weave the #3 round reed just past curve of handle (14 rows).
3. Weave 1 row 3/16" FO reed dyed.
4. Weave 1 row ¾" FF reed.
5. Weave 1 row 3/16" FO reed dyed.
6. Weave 1 row 3/8" FF reed.
7. Twine 3 rows of #3 reed.
8. Trim and tuck all stakes.
9. Work a rewoven braided border:
    - Insert the 40" pieces of well-soaked round reed under the 3 rows of twining.
    - Form scallops by inserting ends of pieces under twining of the 2nd spoke to the right.
    - Start with any pair of round reed pieces and take them behind the pair to the right and out.
    - Take a pair and go under only the pair to the right and up so that you don't go inside. Do this very loosely or the next row will be too tight.
    - Each pair must now trace the path of the pair to the right. First, it will go down to the outside and then to the inside. The braid should stand up straight and not lean in.
10. Make a simple braided border on the inside – take a pair of spokes, go over two and down.

Biscuit Basket

Materials:
2 wrought iron handles
1/4" FO reed
3/8" FF reed
½" FF reed
½" FO reed
5/8" FF reed
¼" FF reed dyed
sea grass

Cutting:
Cut 5 pieces of 5/8" FF reed 23" long
Cut 9 pieces of 5/8" FF reed 18" long

Weaving:
1. Lay the five 23" pieces horizontally.
2. Weave the nine 18" pieces with the center piece going under the first horizontal piece. Bottom should measure 5" x 9 ½".
3. Bend stakes up.
4. Weave alternate rows of ½" FF reed and ¼" FF reed dyed for a total of 9 rows beginning and ending with ½" reed flaring slightly for a finished size of 7" x 12". Weave over the center stakes on all sides on the first row.
5. Place a wrought iron handle on top of each end tucking the center spoke over the center of the handle.
6. Using 3/8" FF reed, make a false rim row going inside the handle.
7. To make an opening for the corners of the liner, trim and tuck as follows:
    - Tuck the 2nd and 4th end stakes in the usual fashion.
    - Cut the ½" weaver on the top row in front of the 1st and 5th end stakes at about the center of the stake. Then bend these stakes down just below the top edge of the false rim and tuck them so that they cover the cut ends of the weavers.
    - Bend the other part of the cut weaver to the side, trim it and tuck the 1st side stake so that it holds the weaver in place and covers it.
    - Trim and tuck the remaining stakes as usual.
8. Use ½" FF reed for inner rim and ½" FO reed for outer rim.
9. Fill with sea grass. If desired, cut the sea grass on insides and outsides of each handle.
10. Lash with ¼" FF reed.
11. Cut a piece of fabric 15" x 17 ½" with pinking shears and pull through openings under rim.

Biscuit Basket with Wood Base

Materials:
5" x 10" wood base
2 wrought iron handles
#2 round reed
1/4" FO reed
3/8" FF reed
½" FF reed
½" FO reed
5/8" FF reed
¼" FF reed dyed
sea grass

Cutting:
Cut 28 pieces of 5/8" FF reed 7" long

Weaving:
1. Insert 9 stakes on long sides of base and 5 stakes on short sides.
2. Twine 1 row with #2 round reed.
3. Bend stakes up.
4. Weave alternate rows of ½" FF reed and ¼" FF reed dyed for a total of 9 rows beginning and ending with
5. ½" reed flaring slightly for a finished size of 7" x 12". Weave outside the center stakes on the long sides on the first row.
6. Place a wrought iron handle on top of each end tucking the center spoke over the center of the handle.
7. Using 3/8" FF reed, make a false rim row going inside the handle.
8. To make an opening for the corners of the liner, trim and tuck as follows:
   - Tuck the 2nd and 4th end stakes in the usual fashion.
   - Cut the ½" weaver on the top row in front of the 1st and 5th end stakes at about the center of the stake. Then bend these stakes down just below the top edge of the false rim and tuck them so that they cover the cut ends of the weavers.
   - Bend the other part of the cut weaver to the side, trim it and tuck the 1st side stake so that it holds the weaver in place and covers it.
   - Trim and tuck the remaining stakes as usual.
9. Use ½" FF reed for inner rim and ½" FO reed for outer rim.
10. Fill with sea grass. If desired, cut the sea grass on insides and outsides of each handle.
11. Lash with ¼" FF reed.
12. Cut a piece of fabric 15" x 17 ½" with pinking shears and pull through openings under rim.

Casserole Caddy

Materials:
10" round wood base
2 ceramic handles
#2 round reed
3/16" FO reed
¼" FF reed
¼" FF reed, dyed or smoked
½" FF reed
5/8" FO reed
sea grass for filler

Cutting:
Cut 32 stakes 5/8" FF reed 6 ½" long

Weaving:
1. Insert the 32 – 5/8"FF stakes evenly around the base. Place two of the stakes on opposite sides of the base in the slot with the smooth sides up. Mark these stakes.
2. Twine 1 row around the base with #2 round reed.
3. Bend stakes up.
4. Weave five rows of ¼" FF weaving the first row outside the marked stakes, 3 rows of ¼" FF dyed reed, 3 rows 1/4" FF reed.
5. Create space for handle as follows: Select 3 stakes on opposite sides of basket having the middle stakes of each of these groups be the marked stakes. Trim and tuck these stakes. The outer stakes of
6. each group must tuck inside and the marked stakes will tuck outside.
7. Weave three more rows of ¼" FF reed starting and stopping at the handle opening. Start the first row behind the end stake. Tuck the end of the second row behind the third stake. Weave the third row like the first.
8. Weave a row of ½" FF reed for false rim putting it through the handles so that they are in the openings that were created for them.
9. Trim and tuck the remaining stakes in the usual fashion except for the stakes next to the handles. Do NOT cut them off--bend them down just below the top edge of the false rim and tuck them to cover the ends of the weavers beside the handles.
10. Use 5/8" FO reed for inner and outer rims and sea grass for filler. Cut the inner rim so that it is exactly the circumference of the top and place the ends in the center of one of the handles. Push the outer rim through the handles but overlap it at the center of one side halfway between the handles.
11. Lash with ¼" FO reed.

Bread Basket

Materials:
¼" FF reed
¼" FO reed
3/8" FF reed
½" FF reed
½" FO reed
¾" FF reed
#3 round reed
Sea grass

Cutting:
Cut 5 stakes of ¾" FF reed 19" long
Cut 4 stakes of ¾" FF reed 22" long
Cut 1 stake of ½" FF reed 22" long
Cut 2 stakes of ½" FF reed 32" long

Weaving:
1. Lay the 4 – 22" long ¾" FF stakes and the 1 – 22" long ½" FF stake horizontally on the table with the ½" FF stake in the center.
2. Weave the 5 – 19" long ¾" stakes vertically with the center stake weaving under the edge.
3. Bottom should be 5" x 8".
4. Bend stakes up.
5. Weave 3 rows of 3/8" FF reed.
6. Twine 2 rows with #3 round reed.
7. Weave 5 rows of ¼" FO.
8. Repeat step 5.
9. Repeat step 4.
10. Trim and tuck.
11. Use ½" FF reed for inner rim, ½" FO reed for outer rim and fill with sea grass.
12. Weave the 2 – 32" long ½" FF pieces weaving diagonally through the bottom. Bring the ends between the rims and bend ends down to form handles
13. Lash rim with ¼' FF reed. Wrap handles with ¼" FF reed.

Apple Basket

Materials:
#2 round reed
¼" FF reed
3/8" FF reed
½" FF reed
1" FF reed
3/8" FO reed
¼" FF reed dyed
#2 round reed dyed
sea grass

Cutting:
Cut 9 pieces of 3/8" FF reed 20" long
Cut 1 piece of ½" FF reed 46" long

Weaving:
1. On the wrong side, mark centers of four of the 20" cut pieces and the 46" cut piece. Also, mark 1" on both sides of center.
2. Lay the 46" piece and the 4 – 20" marked pieces like spokes of a wheel aligning centers.
3. Using a long piece of round reed folded about 6" from the halfway point, begin twining at the 1" marks.
4. (Mark the end of the spoke where twining begins.) Twine six rows.
5. Add the remaining 20" pieces and twine to a diameter of 5".
6. Bend all the stakes to the inside.
7. Weave as follows:
    1 row with 3/8" FF.
    1 row with dyed ¼" reed
    1 row with dyed round reed
    1 row with 1" reed
    1 row with dyed round reed
    1 row with dyed ¼" reed
8. Weave 13 rows with 1/4" reed flaring to 8" at the top. After 3 or 4 rows, if flaring is difficult, turn basket upside down and weave a row or two.
9. Trim and tuck stakes.
10. Push the ends of the long stakes down to form handle. To add stability, add a 15" piece of ½" FF reed on top of existing handle.
11. Use 3/8" FF for inside rim and 3/8" FO for outside rim. Lay a piece of sea grass between the rims beginning on the rim and carrying it up beside the handle and back down to where it began. Repeat sea grass on other side of handle.
12. Wrap the handle with ¼" reed. Wrap 6 times around the handle and then include the sea grass in the wrapping with a piece on each side of the handle. End the wrapping with 6 wraps around the handle.
13. Lash rim with ¼" reed. Leave sea grass free on each side of handle. Trim sea grass ends so they are hidden under the lashing.

Large Apple Basket

Materials:
7" round wood base
#2 round reed
¼" FF reed
3/8" FF reed
5/8" FF reed
5/8" FO reed
¾" FF reed
1" FF reed
#2 round reed, dyed
½" FF reed, dyed
sea grass

Cutting:
Cut 20 pieces 5/8" FF reed 11" long
Cut 1 piece of ¾" FF reed 40" long
Cut 1 piece of ¾" FF reed 20" long

Weaving:
1. Insert the 20 cut pieces of 5/8" FF reed into wooden base.
2. Weave 2 continuous rows of #2 round reed.
3. Bend stakes up and weave 1 row 5/8" FF reed.
4. Weave 1 row ½" FF dyed reed.
5. Weave 1 row dyed #2 round reed.
6. Weave 1 row 1" FF reed.
7. Weave 1 row dyed #2 round reed.
8. Weave 1 row dyed ½" FF reed.
9. Weave 3 rows 3/8" FF reed.
10. Begin to flare the basket and continue weaving 3/8" FF reed until there are 15 rows of 3/8" reed altogether and the diameter is 12". [Suggestion—Weave the 4th row with the basket upside down to get the flare started.]
11. Trim and tuck.
12. Position inner rim of 5/8" FF reed in place.
13. Attach handle by running the ends of the 40" piece of ¾" FF reed under the false rim and the inner rim on opposite sides of the basket. Bring the ends together at the center of the top.
14. Add the 20" piece of ¾" FF reed on top of handle for stability.
15. Position the 5/8" FO outside rim in place.
16. Using 2 pieces of sea grass 38" long, pin center of each piece to the center of the handle. Bring ends around to centers of sides.
17. Wrap handle with ¼" FF reed. Wrap 7 times around the handle and then include the sea grass in the wrapping with a piece on each side of the handle. End by wrapping 7 times around the reed without the sea grass.
18. Lash the rim with ¼" FF reed. Do not include the sea grass in the lashing for about 2" on each side of the handle.

Double Walled Muffin Basket

Materials:
7" round wood base with double groove
#2 round reed
¼" FF reed
¼" FO reed
¼" FO reed smoked
3/8" FF reed
½" FO reed
7/8" FF reed
Sea grass

Cutting:
Cut 22 stakes of 5/8" FF reed 7" long
Cut 22 stakes of ½" FF reed 7" long

Weaving:
1. Insert 5/8" FF stakes in lower groove. Glue in place.
2. Insert ½" FF stakes in upper groove and glue.
3. Twine 3 rows with #2 round reed holding stakes together.
4. Weave 4 rows of ¼" FF reed and 5 rows of 3/8" reed in inner basket with smooth sides facing inside of basket.
5. Weave outer basket as follows: 8 rows ¼" FO reed, 1 row 3/16" FO reed smoked, 1 row 7/8" FF reed, 1 row 3/16" FO smoked, 2 rows ¼" FO reed.
6. Weave 1 row of ¼" FF reed weaving around both sets of stakes.
7. Cut off all stakes on inner basket, trim and tuck outer basket as usual.
8. Using ½" FO reed for inner and outer rims, fill with sea grass and lash with ¼" FO reed.

Chapter 7: Trays

9" x 13" Basket

Materials:
9" x 13" wood base
#2 round reed
1/4" FF reed
1/2" FF reed
1/2" FF reed, smoked or dyed
5/8" FF reed
2 pottery handles

Cutting:
Cut 26 stakes of 5/8" FF reed 5" long
Cut 18 stakes of 1/2" FF reed 5" long

Weaving:
1. Insert eleven 5/8" stakes evenly on long sides of base.
2. Insert one 5/8" stake in each corner.
3. Insert nine 1/2" stakes evenly on short sides of base.
4. Twine 2 rows with #2 round reed or chase weave 2 rows going under the corner stakes on the first row.
5. Bend stakes up.
6. Weave 1 row with 1/4" reed weaving outside the corner stakes.
7. Weave 1 row with 1/2" smoked or dyed FF reed.
8. Weave 2 rows 1/4" FF reed.
9. Create handle opening as follows: Trim and tuck the 3 center stakes on the 9" ends of base. Tuck all three stakes tucking on the outside where needed.
10. Weave two more rows of 1/4" reed. End the first row inside the stakes next to the handle opening. On the next row, wrap the weavers around the stake next to the handle opening and tuck them under the third stake.
11. Weave a false rim row with 1/2" FF reed inserting it through the handles.
12. Trim and tuck the remaining stakes as usual but do not cut off the stakes next to the handle openings. Bend these stakes to the inside and tuck them to cover the ends of weavers.
13. Use 5/8" FF reed for inner and outer rims and sea grass for filler. Insert all of these through handles leaving all ends inside one of the handles.
14. Lash the two sides with 1/4" FF reed.

Round Tray Basket

Materials:
15" round wood base
#3 round reed
3/16" FO reed smoked
¼" FO reed
½" FF reed
5/8" FO reed
5/8" FF reed
sea grass
3/8" braided sea grass

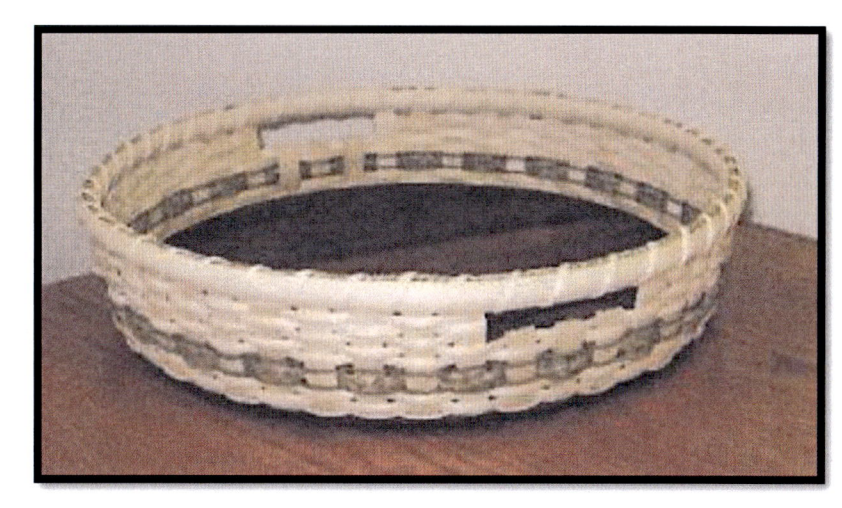

Cutting:
Cut 48 stakes of 5/8" FF reed 5 ½" long

Weaving:
1. Insert the 48 stakes evenly around the base. Insert all stakes with smooth sides down except 2 stakes on opposite sides of the base which should have smooth sides up.
2. Twine 1 row of #3 round reed.
3. Bend stakes up.
4. Weave 2 rows of ¼" FO reed (weaving outside the stakes with the smooth side up on the first row), 1 row of 3/16" FO smoked reed, 1 row braided sea grass, 1 row 3/16" FO smoked reed, 2 rows ¼" FO reed.
5. Create handle openings as follows: Tuck the 2 stakes with smooth sides up to the outside. Tuck the stakes on each side of them to the inside.
6. Weave 3 more rows of ¼" FO reed starting and stopping at the handle openings. Start the first and third rows behind the end stake. Tuck the end of the second row behind the third stake.
7. Weave a false rim row of ½" FF reed.
8. Trim and tuck. DO NOT cut off the stakes next to the openings. Tuck them to cover ends.
9. Use 5/8" FO reed for inner and outer rims, fill with sea grass and lash with ¼" FO reed wrapping around the rim four times above the handle openings.

Oblong Tray Basket with Rosewood Handles

Materials:
11" x 16" oblong wood base
3/16" FO reed
¼" FF reed
3/8" FF reed
3/8" FF reed dyed
5/8" FF reed
5/8" FO reed
Sea grass
1 pair rosewood handles

Cutting:
Cut 48 stakes of 5/8" FF reed 5 1/2" long

Weaving:
1. Insert one 5/8" stakes in each corner of base, 13 stakes on long sides and 9 on ends. The center stake on each end should have the smooth side up.
2. Bend stakes up and weave 2 rows of 3/16" FO weaving the first row outside the corners and bringing stakes to a nearly vertical position at the end of two rows..
3. Weave 1 rows of ¼" FF reed, 1 row 3/8" FF reed dyed, 2 rows ¼" FF reed.
4. Create handle openings as follows: Tuck the 2 end stakes with smooth sides up to the outside. Tuck the stakes on each side of them to the inside.
5. Weave 3 more rows of ¼" FF reed starting and stopping at the handle openings. Start the first and third rows behind the end stake. Tuck the end of the second row behind the third stake.
6. Weave a false rim row of 3/8" FF reed inserting it through the handles.
7. Trim and tuck. Do not cut off the stakes beside the handles. Bend these stakes down and tuck them to cover the cut ends of the weavers.
8. Use 5/8" FF reed for inner rim and 5/8" FO for outer rim. Go through handles with both.
9. Fill with sea grass and lash with ¼" FO reed.

Small Round Tray (12" Or 13")

13" Version:

Materials:
13" round wood base
#3 round reed
3/16" FO reed
¼" FF reed
¼" FO reed
3/8" FO reed
5/8" FF reed
½" FF reed smoked
Sea grass

Cutting:
Cut 40 stakes of 5/8' FF reed 4" long

Weaving:
1. Insert stakes evenly in base.
2. Twine 1 row with #3 round reed.
3. Weave 2 rows of ¼" FF or FO reed..
4. Weave 1 row ½" FF reed smoked.
5. Weave 3 rows ¼" FF or FO reed and 1 row ¼" FF reed.
6. Trim and tuck
7. Use 3/8" FO reed for outer rim and inner rim, fill with sea grass and lash with ¼" FO reed.

12" Version:

Materials:
12" round wood base
#3 round reed
3/16" FO reed
¼" FF reed
¼" FO reed
3/8" FO reed
5/8" FF reed
½" FF reed smoked
Sea grass

Cutting:
Cut 36 stakes of 5/8' FF reed 3 ½" long

Weaving:
Weave same as above except in step 5 begin by weaving 2 rows instead of 3.

Chapter 8: Storage Baskets

Storage Basket

Materials
#2 round reed
3/16" FO reed
¼" FF reed, smoked
3/8" FF reed
½" FF reed
½" FO reed
5/8" FF reed, smoked
sea grass
2 wrought iron handles

Cutting
Cut 18 stakes of ½" FF reed 34" long
Cut 8 fillers of 3/8" FF reed 14" long

Weaving
1. Mark centers of some of the 34" stakes and lay 9 of them horizontally on the table.
2. Mark centers of some of the fillers and ay the fillers between the stakes.
3. Weave the remaining stakes vertically beginning in the center by weaving under the horizontal stakes and over the fillers. Square bottom to 8.5" x 8.5".
4. Trim, split and tuck ends of fillers under the second row of stakes from each side.
5. Twine 1 row with #2 round reed.
6. Bend stakes up and weave 4 rows of 3/8" FF reed.
7. Weave 2 rows ¼" smoked reed, 1 row 5/8" smoked reed, and 2 more rows ¼" smoked reed.
8. Weave 8 rows of 3/8" FF reed.
9. Do not cut spokes. Use ½" FF reed for inner rim and ½" FO reed for outer rim. Double lash with 3?16" FO reed lashing a wrought iron handle on the three center stakes on opposite sides.
10. Weave 6 rows of 3/8" FF reed pulling in slightly and making sure to keep equal distance between the stakes.
11. Trim and tuck.
12. Use ½" FF reed for inner rim, ½' for outer rim and fill with sea grass.
13. Double lash with 3/16" FO reed.

Storage Basket with Wood Base

Materials
9" square wood base
#2 round reed
3/16" FO reed
¼" FF reed, smoked
½" FF reed
5/8" FF reed
5/8" FO reed
5/8" FF reed, smoked
sea grass
2 wrought iron handles

Cutting
Cut 28 stakes of 5/8" FF reed 13" long
Cut 4 stakes of ½" FF reed 13" long
Cut 4 pieces of ½" FO reed 8" long

Weaving
1. Insert 7 – 5/8" stakes evenly on each side of base and 1 – ½" stake in each corner.
2. Twine 1 row with #2 round reed.
3. Bend stakes up and weave 4 rows of ½" FF reed.
4. Weave 2 rows ¼" smoked reed, 1 row 5/8" smoked reed, and 2 more rows ¼" smoked reed.
5. Weave 7 rows of ½" FF reed.
6. Do not cut spokes. Use 5/8" FF reed for inner rim and 5/8" FO reed for outer rim. Double lash with 3/16" FO reed lashing a wrought iron handle on the three center stakes on opposite sides.
7. Weave 5 rows of ½" FF reed pulling in slightly.
8. Trim and tuck.
9. Use 5/8" FF reed for inner rim, 5/8" FO reed for outer rim and fill with sea grass.
10. Double lash with 3/16" FO reed.

Large Storage Basket

Materials:
Wood base 13" x 18"
#3 round reed
3/16" FO reed
¼" FF reed
½" FF reed
5/8" FF reed
5/8" FF reed dyed
5/8" FO reed
¾" FF reed
Sea grass
Wrought iron side handles (2)

Cutting:
Cut 52 stakes of ¾" FF reed 11" long
Cut 4 stakes of 5/8" FF reed 11" long
Cut 4 stakes of 5/8" FO reed 10" long

Weaving:
1. Insert fifteen ¾" stakes on long sides, eleven stakes on short sides and four 5/8" stakes in corners.
2. Twine 1 row with #3 round reed.
3. Bend stakes up.
4. Weave 3 rows with ½" FF reed weaving the first row outside the corners. After 3 rows, push the four 5/8" FO stakes into the corners on top of the 5/8" FF reed.
5. Weave 4 rows of ½" FF reed. (Total rows – 7)
6. Weave 1 row of sea grass, 3 rows 5/8" FF reed dyed, 1 row of sea grass.
7. Weave 2 rows ½" FF reed. On the second r, weave another piece of ½" FF reed over the original piece on the ends of the basket only.
8. Weave 3 rows of ½" FF reed.
9. Trim and tuck.
10. Insert the end of an 18" piece of ¼" FO reed between the layers of the double-woven row on the end of the basket between the 4th and 5th stakes. Wrap it over the wrought iron handle and behind the next stake for the next three stakes. Then reverse direction making X's over the handle. Tuck the end between the layers. Repeat on the opposite end of the basket.

Medium Gathering Basket

The bottom of this basket is 10" x 18".

Materials:
10 x 14 D handle
1/4" FO reed
½" FF reed
5/8" FF reed
5/8" FO reed
3/4" FF dyed reed
sea grass

Cutting:
Cut 7 pieces 5/8" FF reed 40" long
Cut 12 pieces 5/8" FF reed 32" long

Weaving:
1. Mark centers of base of handle and all cut pieces on rough side.
2. Lay the long stakes vertically on the table with marked side up.
3. Weave the handle across the center marks with the first and last spokes over the handle.
4. Weave the shorter stakes across the long stakes with half of them on each side of the handle. Bottom should measure 10" x 18".
5. Bend the stakes up and weave 9 rows of 5/8" FF reed with the first row outside the handle.
6. Weave 1 row of sea grass, 1 row of 3/4" FF dyed reed, 1 row of sea grass, 3 rows of 5/8" FF reed and 1 row of ½" FF reed.
7. Trim and tuck.
8. Use 5/8" FF reed for inner rim and 5/8" FO reed for outer rim. Fill with sea grass.
9. Lash with 1/4" FO reed.

Large Gathering Basket

This basket may be made 30" long or 36" long. The numbers in parentheses are for the 36" size.

Materials:
10 x 20 D handle
1/4" FO reed
½" FF reed
5/8" FF reed
5/8" FO reed
1" FF dyed reed
sea grass

Cutting:
Cut 7 pieces of 5/8" FF reed 58" (64") long
Cut 20 (24) pieces of 5/8" FF reed 38" long

Weaving:
1. Mark centers of base of handle and all cut pieces on rough side.
2. Lay the long stakes vertically on the table with marked side up.
3. Weave the handle across the center marks with the first and last spokes over the handle.
4. Weave the shorter stakes across the long stakes with half of them on each side of the handle. Bottom should measure 10" x 30" (36").
5. Bend the stakes up and weave 11 rows of 5/8" FF reed with the first row outside the handle.
6. Weave 1 row of sea grass, 1 row of 1" FF dyed reed and 1 row of sea grass.
7. Weave 3 rows of 5/8" FF reed and 1 row of ½" FF reed.
8. Trim and tuck.
9. Use 5/8" FF reed for inner rim and 5/8" FO reed for outer rim. Fill with sea grass.
10. Lash with 1/4" FO reed.

Round Carry-All Basket

Materials:
12" round wood base
#2 round reed
3/8" FF reed
¾" FF reed
5/8" FO reed
sea grass
1 pair 10" leather handles

Cutting:
Cut 36 stakes of ¾" FF reed 12" long

Weaving:
1. Insert stakes evenly in base.
2. Twine once around base with #2 round reed.
3. Bend stakes up.
4. Weave 22 rows of 3/8" FF reed flaring slightly to a diameter of 14"
5. The false rim row will also be 3/8" FF reed but the handles must be attached to it. Slip the reed through the loops of the handles. Place the first end behind any spoke that will be cut off and the other end behind the 4th spoke from that one which is a spoke that will also be cut off. Skip 13 spokes and repeat the handle placement with the other handle.
6. Trim and tuck.
7. Use 5/8" FO reed for inner and outer rims, fill with sea grass (cut around handles) and double lash with 3/16" FO reed.

Round Carry-All Basket with Continuous Weave

Materials:
12" round wood base
#3 round reed
¼" FO reed
3/8" FF reed
½" FF reed
¾" FF reed
5/8" FF reed
5/8" FO reed
sea grass
1 pair 10" leather handles

Cutting:
Cut 35 stakes of ¾" FF reed 13" long

Weaving:
1. Insert stakes evenly in base.
2. Twine once around base with #3 round reed.
3. Bend stakes up.
4. Weave 19 rows of ½" FF reed flaring slightly to a diameter of 14". This will be continuous weave so taper the ends. Weave a twill weave of over 2, under 1.
5. The false rim row will be woven over 1, under 1 of 3/8" FF reed but the handles must be attached to it. Slip the reed through the loops of the handles. Place the first end behind any spoke that will be cut off and the other end behind the 4th spoke from that one which is a spoke that will also be cut off. Skip 13 spokes and repeat the handle placement with the other handle. Also insert sea grass through handles.
6. Trim and tuck.
7. Use 5/8" FF reed for inner rim and 5/8" FO reed for outer rim, fill with sea grass and lash with ¼" FO reed (3.5 yds).

Square-Bottom Carryall Basket

Materials:
11" square wood base
3/16" FO reed
½" FF reed
½" FF reed, smoked
5/8" FF reed
5/8" FO reed
4 – 1 ¾" ball feet
2 bushel handles

Cutting:
Cut 40 stakes 15" long of 5/8" FF reed.

Weaving:
1. Insert 9 stakes on each side of base and one stake in each corner.
2. Weave one row of 3/16" FO reed keeping stakes flat. Bend stakes up gently and weave 3 more rows of 3/16" FO reed. (4 rows altogether)
3. Weave two rows of 5/8" FF reed, 3 rows ½" FF smoked reed, (3 rows 5/8" FF reed, 3 rows smoked reed) twice, 2 rows 5/8" FF reed, 1 row ½" FF reed. When weaving bring sides out so that the diameter at the top is 16-17".
4. Trim and tuck.
5. Use 5/8" FO reed for inner and outer rims and fill with sea grass.
6. Before lashing, insert handles centered on opposite sides of basket between false rim and outer rim. There should be 5 stakes between the sides of the handles.
7. Lash with ¼" FO reed.

Laundry Basket

Materials:
17" x 25" wood base
#3 round reed
¼" FO reed
3/8" FF reed
5/8" FF reed
5/8" FO reed
7/8" FF reed
1" FF reed
Sea grass
1 pair 10" leather handles

Cutting:
Cut 52 stakes of 7/8" FF reed 16" long
Cut 4 stakes of 5/8" FF reed 16" long
Cut 4 pieces of 5/8" FO reed 12" long

Weaving:
1. Insert one 5/8" stakes in each corner of base, 15 – 7/8" FF stakes on long sides and 11 – 7/8" FF on short sides.
2. Twine 1 row around base with #3 round reed.
3. Bend stakes up.
4. Weave 3 rows of 5/8" FF reed weaving the first row outside the corners.
5. Soak the pieces of 5/8" FO reed, taper one end of each and push them into the corners on top of the 5/8" FF reed.
6. Weave 7 more rows of 5/8" FF reed, 3 rows of 1" FF reed, and 5 rows of 5/8" FF reed.
7. Weave a false rim row of 3/8" FF reed.

> Note—the false rim row may be inserted through the handles which will hide the bottoms of the handles between the rim rows. Or the outside rim may be inserted through the handles which will put the bottoms of the handles on the outside of the basket. In either case, the sea grass should be inserted in the handles.

8. Trim and tuck
9. Use 5/8" FF reed for inner rim and 5/8" FO for outer rim. Fill with sea grass and lash with ¼" FO reed.

Chapter 9: Hanging Baskets

Wall Basket

Materials:
5" wire heart hanger
#2 round reed
#3 round reed
¼" FF or FO reed, dyed or smoked
3/8" FF reed
½" FF reed
1" ash or maple strip

Cutting:
From ½" FF reed cut:
- a) 3 horizontal stakes 30" long
- b) 9 vertical stakes 26" long
- c) 2 fillers 16" long

From #2 round cut 24 pieces 22" long

Weaving:
1. Lay the three horizontal stakes on the table and mark centers.
1. Place the two fillers between the stakes and mark centers.
2. Mark centers on the vertical stakes and weave one through the center marks on the horizontal stakes going under the horizontals and over the fillers.
3. Weave remaining vertical stakes with four on each side of the center.
4. Push the horizontal stakes and fillers tightly together. The base should measure 2 ½" x 8" approx.
5. Cut and tuck the fillers.
6. Twine around the base with #3 round reed for one row. (Start at a corner.)
7. Bend the stakes up and continue twining for four more rows.
8. Weave sides as follows:
   - 5 rows 3/8" FF reed, weave first row over all center stakes.
   - 1 row ¼" FF or FO reed, dyed or smoked
   - 1 row ash or maple strip
   - 1 row ¼" FF or FO reed, dyed or smoked
   - 3 rows 3/8" FF reed
9. Using a 2 yard piece of 3/8" FF reed, start behind the middle stake on the side and weave across the back to the other center side stake, turn and continue weaving decreasing one stake on each side each row until a total of seven rows have been woven on the back. Tuck end of weaver behind stakes.
10. To form rim, twine three rows with #3 round reed.
11. Cut and tuck stakes on front and sides of basket.
12. Soak the pieces of #2 round reed for several minutes. Then insert a piece hairpin style with one end under the triple weave on any stake and the other end under the triple weave on the stake that is the second one to the right. Pull the ends up so they are even and there is a scallop at the lower edge of the top row of ½" reed. Continue around the basket.

13. Cut center back stake even with twining and insert wire hanger.
14. Trim and tuck back stakes to the back.
15. Weave braid as follows: (Be sure to braid in front of the wire hanger.)
    - Grasp one pair of round reed, bring it behind the pair to the right and down to the outside of the basket. Repeat this around the basket inserting the last pair through the first loop formed.
    - Insert one pair into the top of the loop on the right and push down to the inside. The last pair will be inserted into the first loop formed.
    - Repeat the above two steps to complete the braided edge.
16. After the basket dries, trim ends of round reed.

Wall Basket with Wood Base

Materials:
2.5" x 8" wood base
5" wire heart hanger
#2 round reed
#3 round reed
¼" FF or FO reed, dyed or smoked
3/8" FF reed
½" FF reed
1" ash or maple strip

Cutting:
From ½" FF reed cut:
- d) 9 stakes 13" long for back
- e) 9 stakes 9" long for front
- f) 3 stakes 10" long for ends

From #2 round cut 24 pieces 22" long

Weaving:
1. Insert stakes in base placing nine 9" stakes in front, three 10" stakes on each end and nine 13" stakes in back.
2. Twine around the base with #3 round reed for one row. (Start at a corner.)
3. Bend the stakes up and continue twining for four more rows.
4. Weave sides as follows:
   - 5 rows 3/8" FF reed, weave first row over all center stakes.
   - 1 row ¼" FF or FO reed, dyed or smoked
   - 1 row ash or maple strip
   - 1 row ¼" FF or FO reed, dyed or smoked
   - 3 rows 3/8" FF reed
5. Using a 2 yard piece of 3/8" FF reed, start behind the middle stake on the side and weave across the back to the other center side stake, turn and continue weaving decreasing one stake on each side each row until a total of seven rows have been woven on the back.
6. To form rim, twine three rows with #3 round reed.
7. Cut and tuck stakes on front and sides of basket.
8. Soak the pieces of #2 round reed for several minutes. Then insert a piece hairpin style with one end under the triple weave on any stake and the other end under the triple weave on the stake that is the second one to the right. Pull ends up so they are even with a scallop at the bottom. Repeat around.
9. Trim and tuck back stakes to the back.
10. Weave braid as follows:
11. Grasp one pair of round reed, bring it behind the pair to the right and down to the outside of the basket. Repeat this around the basket inserting the the last pair through the first loop formed.
12. Insert one pair into the top of the loop on the right and push down to the inside. The last pair will be inserted into the first loop formed.
13. Repeat the above two steps to complete 3rd and 4th rows of braid. NOTE: Insert tips of handle after the 3rd row and catch handle in the looping on the 4th row. Insert ends to the back where possible. After the basket dries, trim ends of round reed.

Plaid Wall Basket

Materials:
5" half-round wood base
#2 round reed
1/4" FF reed, natural and dyed
3/16" FF reed
3/16" FO reed
1/2" FF reed
1/2" FO reed
sea grass

Cutting:
Cut 20 stakes of 1/4" FF reed natural 8" long
Cut 10 stakes of 1/4" FF reed dyed (color 1) 8" long
Cut 10 stakes of 1/4" FF reed dyed (color 2) 8" long
Cut 1 piece of 1/2" FF reed 18" long for handle.

Weaving:
1. Insert the 40 stakes into the base beginning with 4 dyed stakes in the center of the flat side of the base and 4 natural stakes on each side of the dyed ones. The four dyed stakes should have two stakes of each color together. Continue inserting stakes into the base around the curve following the same color sequence established on the flat side.
2. Begin all weaving on the flat side. Weave 1 round with #2 round reed.
3. Weave one round with 3/16" FF reed.
4. Bend stakes up.
5. Begin weaving plaid by weaving one row of 1/4" FF going over 2 nat stakes, under 2 dyed stakes, over 2 dyed stakes, under 2 nat stakes, over 2 nat stakes, etc.
6. Continue to weave under 2 and over 2 for the next 3 rows moving one stake to the right before beginning each row.
7. On the fifth row move one stake to the left before beginning to weave and continue in this manner for rows 6, 7 and 8. On these rows, weave the first 2 rows with color 1 and the second 2 rows with color 2.
8. Repeat rows 1 through 8 for rows 9 through 16.
9. Repeat rows 1 through 5 for rows 17 through 21 using 1/4" FF nat reed (row 21 is false rim).
10. Trim and tuck.
11. Use 1/2" FF reed for inner rim and 1/2" FO reed for outer rim. Fill with sea grass.
12. Before lashing, bend handle about 1/2" from center and insert under false rim on one side of the dyed reed on the flat side. Bend the longer end up about 1/4" and insert under the false rim on the opposite side of the dyed reed. Bring the other end down to meet this end. Trim the stakes where necessary to get the handle inserted.
13. Lash with 3/16" FO reed making an "X" over the handle ends.
14. Wrap handle with 1/4" FF reed.

Weed Basket

The instructions are given for this basket in two sizes. Numbers for the larger basket are in parentheses. The smaller is basket is 5" wide at the bottom, 6" tall and has a 4" diameter at the top. The larger is 6" wide at the bottom, 8" tall and has a diameter of 5" at the top.

Materials:
3/16" FO reed
¼" FF reed
¼" FF reed, dyed
3/8" FF reed
½" FF reed
½" FF reed, dyed
5/8" FF reed
#2 round reed
sea grass

Cutting:
Cut 7 (9) pieces of ½" FF reed 16" (18") long.

Weaving
1. Mark centers of the ½" FF pieces and lay them vertically on the table ¼" apart.
2. Beginning about ¼" below the center, twine across the stakes. Turn at the end of the row and twine back. Twine 4 rows altogether ending at the 5th (7th) stake on the 4th row. The 5th (7th) stake must be split to function as 2 stakes temporarily.
3. Taper the last 3" of a ¼" FF weaver and begin weaving at the split. Weave 16 (20) continuous rows ending by tapering the last 3" above the original taper.
4. Weave 3 stop-start rows of dyed reed—one ¼" FF, one ½" FF, one ¼" FF. On these rows and the following rows, treat the split reed as one piece from here on.
5. Weave 4 rows of ¼" FF reed.
6. Trim and tuck.
7. Using a 5" (8") piece of ¼" (3/8") FF reed, make a handle by tucking the ends under the second row of weavers in front of the split reed and the corresponding piece on the other side of the center. Bend the ends up so that they will be under the rim.
8. Use ½" (5/8") FF reed for inner and outer rims. Fill with sea grass and lash with 3/16" FO reed.

Doorknob Basket

Materials:
2 ¾" x 6 ½" wood base 3/8" thick
#2 round reed
3/16" FO reed
¼" FF reed dyed
3/8" FF reed
½" FF reed
5/8" FF reed
Sea grass
Bushel handle, 2 ½", cl notch

Cutting:
Cut 14 stakes of 5/8" FF reed 10" long
Cut 2 stakes of ½" FF reed 10" long

Weaving:
1. Insert the 16 stakes in the base, 5 on each side and 3 on each end with the ½" stakes in the center of the end.
2. Twine 1 rows with #2 round reed.
3. Bend stakes up.
4. Weave 5 rows of ½" FF reed, 5 rows of ¼" FF reed dyed, 4 rows ½" FF reed, 1 row 3/8" FF reed.
5. Trim and tuck.
6. Insert ends of handle under several rows on the outside of the back of the basket.
7. Use ½' FF for inner and outer rims and fill with sea grass.
8. Double lash with ¼" FO reed.

Chapter 10: Purses and Totes

Basket Purse #1

Materials:
Wooden base - 3 1/2" x 8 3/4"
#2 round reed
3/16" FO reed
1/4" FO reed, dyed or smoked
1/4" FF reed
3/8" FF reed
1/2" FO reed
sea grass
1 pair of leather handles

Cutting:
Cut 48 stakes of 1/4" dyed FO reed 9" long

Weaving:
1. Insert stakes evenly into wood base--do not dampen.
2. Chase weave 2 rows of #2 round reed.
3. Dampen stakes and bend up.
4. Weave twill pattern as follows:
    - With 1/4" FF reed weave over 3, under 2, over 1, under 2 repeating around the row.
    - Move one stake to the right and weave same as above.
    - Continue the pattern until there are 8 rows of ZIG.
    - Move one stake to the left on each row for the next 8 rows to form ZAG.
    - Repeat these 16 rows for a total of 32 rows.
5. Weave a false rim row of 3/8" FF reed weave over 1, under 1 if possible.
6. Trim and tuck.
7. Insert rim pieces and sea grass into loops of handles before placing on basket.
8. Lash with 3/16" FO reed making X over handles.

Basket Purse #2

Materials:
4"x10" shaped wood base
#2 round reed
1/4" FO reed
3/16" FO reed
3/16" FO reed dyed burgundy
3/16" FO reed dyed navy
3/8" FF reed
1/2" FF reed
1/2" FO reed
sea grass
1 pair of leather handles

Cutting:
Cut 24 stakes of 1/2" FF reed 12" long

Weaving:
1. Insert stakes.
2. Twine 2 rows with #2 round reed.
3. Weave 18 rows with 1/4" FO reed.
    Circumferences:
        Row 6 - 28"
        Row 18 - 27"
        Row 23 - 26 1/2"
        Row 28 - 25"
4. Weave 9 rows of 3/16" dyed reed--3 rows navy, 3 rows burgundy, 3 rows navy or vice versa.
5. Weave 5 rows 1/4" FO reed.
6. Weave 1 row 3/8" FF reed.
7. Trim and tuck.
8. Using 1/2" FO reed, put inner rim in place with clothes pins.
9. Insert 1/2" FO outer rim and sea grass through loops in handles and pin in place with clothes pins.
10. Double lash with 3/16" FO reed.

Basket Purse #3

Materials:
4"x10" shaped wood base
#2 round reed
1/4" FF reed
1/4" FF reed dyed
11/64" FO reed
3/8" FF reed
1/2" FF reed
1/2" FO reed
sea grass
1 pair of 20" fabric/leather handles

Cutting:
Cut 24 stakes of 1/2" FF reed 10" long
Cut 6 overlays of 1/4" dyed reed (optional)

Weaving:
1. Insert stakes evenly in base.
2. Twine 2 rows with #2 round reed.
3. Weave 20 rows with 1/4" FF reed weaving over the center stakes. After the third row the circumference should be approx 27". After third row insert the overlays on top of the center stakes on both front and back and on the second stakes away from these on both right and left. Continue weaving straight up after that so that the circumference remains 27".
4. Weave 1 row 3/8" FF reed slipping it through the handles. Handles should lie on top of stakes so that there are 5 stakes between the handles on the front and back and five stakes between around the ends.
5. DO NOT CUT THE STAKES. Use 1/2" FO reed for outer rim threading it through handles and 1/2" FF reed for inner rim. Cut off extra length of overlays.
6. Double lash with 11/64" FO.
7. Weave 7 more rows pushing spokes inward slightly.
8. Weave a false rim row of 3/8"FF
9. Trim and tuck.
10. Use 1/2" FF reed for inner rim, 1/2" FO for outer rim and sea grass for filler.
11. Double lash with 3/16" FO reed.

Basket Purse #4

Materials:
4"x10" shaped wood base
#2 round reed
3/16" FO reed
1/4" FF reed
3/8" FF reed
1/2" FF reed
1/2" FO reed
#2 round reed
#2 round reed, smoked
sea grass
1 pair of 15" leather handles

Cutting:
Cut 24 stakes of 1/2" FF reed 10" long
Cut 24 weavers of 3/16" FO reed 13" long

Weaving:
1. Insert stakes evenly in base.
2. Twine 2 rows with #2 round reed.
3. Weave 8 rows of ¼" FF reed weaving the 1st row outside the ends.
4. Triple twine 2 rows with #2 smoked round reed doing a step-up.
5. Diagonal weave the 24 3/16" FO weavers.
6. Repeat step 4.
7. Weave 8 rows of ¼" FF reed.
8. Weave a false rim row of 3/8"FF
9. Trim and tuck.
10. Use 1/2" FF reed, put inner rim in place with clothes pins.
11. Insert ½" FO outer rim and sea grass through loops in handles and pin in place.
12. Double lash with 3/16" FO reed.

Lining (optional):
1. Cut two pieces of fabric 14" x 28".
2. Fold both pieces into 14" squares with folds at lower edge.
3. Cut out corners as shown at right.
4. Sew side seams in both leaving an opening ing the lining.
5. Clip corners and sew the opening to make a flat bottom.
6. With bag right-side out and lining wrong-side out, pull lining over bag and sew top edges together.
7. Turn through opening and sew opening shut.
8. Put 10 metal eyelets evenly around top and insert drawstring.

Basket Purse #5

Materials:
4 x 10 shaped wood base
#1 round reed
3/16" FO reed
¼" FF reed
3/8" FF reed dyed
½" FF reed
½" FO reed
Sea grass
1 pr. 15" leather handles

Cutting:
Cut 40 stakes of 3/8" FF dyed reed 10" long

Weaving:
1. Insert stakes evenly in base marking center stakes (CS) on sides and end stakes (ES).
2. Twine 2 rows w/#1 round reed.
3. Weaving with 3/16" FO reed, weave as follows always beginning at a CS:
   - R1 - *weave o(over)3 (CS and one on each side), u(under)2, o2, u2, o2, u1, o2, u2, o2, u2*, repeat between *s.
   - R2 - *u CS, o2, u2, o2, u2, o3, u2, o2, u2, o2*, repeat.
   - R3 - *u3, (CS and one on each side), o2, u2, o2, u2, o1, u2, o2, u2, o2*, repeat.
   - R4 - *o CS, u2, o2, u2, o2, u3, o2, u2, o2, u2*, repeat.
   - Repeat the above 4-row sequence 5 times (20 rows).
   - R21- same as R1.
   - R22- same as R2.
   - R23 - *oCS, u1, o2, u2, o2, u2, o1, u2, o2, u2, o2, u1*, repeat.
   - R24 - *uCS, o1, u1, o2, u2, o2, u3, o2, u2, o2, u1, o1*, repeat.
   - R25 - *oCS, u1, o1, u1, o2, u2, o2, u1, o2, u2, o2, u1, o1, u1*, repeat.
   - R26 - *uCS, o1, u1, o1, u1, o2, u2, o3, u2, o2, u1, o1, u1*, repeat.
   - R27 - *oCS, u1, o1, u1, o1, u1, o2, u2, o1, u2, o2, u1, o1, u1, o1, u1*, repeat.
   - R28 - *uCS, o1, u1, o1, u1, o1, u1, o2, u3, o2, u1, o1, u1, o1, u1, o1*, repeat.
   - R29 - *oCS, u1, o1, u1, o1, u1, o1, u1, o2, u1, o2, u1, o1, u1, o1, u1, o1, u1*, repeat.
   - R30 - *uCS, [o1, u1] 4x, o3, [u1, o1] 4x*, repeat.
   - R31 – oCS, u1, *[o1, u1]* repeat around.
4. Weave R32 with ¼" FF reed.
   - R32 - uCS, o1, *[u1, o1]* repeat around.
5. Trim and tuck.
6. Use ½" FF for inner rim, ½" FO for outer rim and fill with sea grass. Insert outer rim and sea grass through loops in handle.
7. Single lash with 3/16" FO reed.

Purse #6 — Lightning Purse

Materials:
4" x 9" shaped wood base
#2 round reed
3/16" FO reed
¼" FF reed
¼" FF reed smoked
½" FF reed
3/8" FF reed
½" FO reed
Sea grass
1 pr. 15" leather handles

Cutting:
Cut 48 stakes of ¼" FF reed smoked 11" long

Weaving:
1. Insert stakes evenly in base as follows: mark centers of sides and ends of base, insert a stake on each side of each mark and then insert remaining stakes evenly between. Glue in place.
2. Twine 2 rows of #2 round reed.
3. Weave 1 row of 3/16" FO reed weaving twill pattern of over 3, under 2, over 1, under 2.
4. With ¼" FF reed, weave the same twill pastern moving 1 stake to the right.
5. Continue twill pattern moving 1 stake to the right until there are 6 rows of twill. Then move to the left each row for 4 rows (10 rows altogether). Repeat this entire sequence again for a total of 20 rows of twill. The repeat the first 6 rows on more time—26 rows of twill.
6. Weave a row of 3/8" FF reed weaving over 2, under 2.
7. Trim and tuck.
8. Use ½" FF reed for inner rim, ½" FO reed for outer rim and fill with sea grass. Insert sea grass and outer rim through handles and lash with 3/16" FO reed.

Tote/Purse Basket with Leather Handles

Materials:
3½ x 11½ wood base w/legs
#2 round reed
¼" FF reed
¼" FO reed
3/8" FF reed
½" FF reed
5/8" FF reed
5/8" FO reed
¾" FF reed
Sea grass
1 pair of 15" leather handles

Cutting:
Cut 14 stakes of ¾" FF reed 11" long
Cut 10 stakes of ½" FF reed 11" long

Weaving:
1. Insert a ½" FF stake in each corner and 3 - ½" FF stakes on each end. Insert 7 – ¾" FF stakes on the sides.
2. Glue all stakes in place.
3. Twine 1 rows with #2 round reed.
4. Bend stakes up.
5. Weave 1 row of ½" FF reed weaving outside the corner stakes.
6. Weave 3 rows ¼" FF reed
   1 row ½" FF reed
   3 rows ¼" FF reed
   1 row ¾" FF reed
   1 row ¼" FF reed
   1 row ¾" FF reed
   3 rows ¼" FF reed
   1 row ½" FF reed
   3 rows ¼" FF reed
   1 row ½" FF reed
   2 rows ¼" FF reed
   1 row 3/8" FF reed

   Note: Pull the weavers in slightly as you go up to give the basket a little shape.

7. Trim and tuck.
8. Use 5/8" FO for outer rim and 5/8" FF for inner rim, fill with sea grass. Insert outer rim and sea grass through loops in handle.
9. Lash with ¼" FO reed.

Tote Basket

Materials:
10" square open-notched handle
#2 round reed
3/16" FO reed
3/8" FF reed
½" FF reed
½" FO reed
5/8" FF reed
3/8" FF reed dyed red or burgundy
½" FF reed dyed navy
rush for filler

Cutting:
Cut 9 stakes of 5/8" FF reed 28" long
Cut 5 stakes of 5/8" FF reed 32" long
Cut 4 fillers of 5/8" FF reed 12" long

Weaving:
2. Mark centers of some of the stakes and fillers.
3. Lay the 5 - 32" stakes horizontally on the table.
4. Lay a 28" stake vertically at the center.
5. Lay the fillers on top of the vertical stake so that they lie horizontally between the 32" stakes.
6. Weave four of the 28" stakes on each side of center.
7. Base should be 6" x 10".
8. Trim fillers to make them even with basket base.
9. Bend stakes up.
10. Weave sides as follows:
    - 4 rows ½" FF reed
    - Twine 3 rows with #2 round reed.
    - 1 row navy, 1 row red, 1 row navy, 1 row red, 1 row navy.
    - Twine 3 rows with #2 round reed.
    - 4 rows ½" FF reed
    - 1 row 3/8" FF reed (false rim)
11. Trim and tuck.
12. Use ½" FF reed for inner rim, ½" FO reed for outer rim and fill with rush.
13. Insert handle between inner rim and false rim.
14. Lash with 3/16" FO reed.
15. Add crisscross trim as follows:

- Insert the end of a piece of 3/16" FO reed under the left side of a stake just above the first set of twining.
- Bend the reed, bring it to the right and insert the other end of the 3/16" reed under the next stake on the right pulling it through from right to left so that it is at the top of the red weaver.
- Bend the reed, bring it to the right and insert the end under the next stake pulling it through from right to left so that it is at the bottom of the navy weaver.
- Repeat the last two steps around the basket and then repeat this trim on the upper rows of red and navy as shown in the picture.

Tote Basket with Shaker Tape Handles

Materials:
1 ¾ yards of Shaker tape
3½ x 11½ wood tote base
#2 round reed
¼" FF reed
¼" FO reed
½" FF reed
½" FO reed
7/8" FF reed
Sea grass

Cutting:
Cut 16 stakes of 7/8" FF reed 14" long
Cut 8 stakes of ½" FF reed 14" long
Cut 4 stakes of ½" FO reed 10" long

Weaving:
1. Insert a ½" FF stake in each corner and 2 - ½" FF stakes on each end with a 7/8" FF stake in the center of each end. Insert 7 - 7/8" FF stakes on the sides.
2. Glue all stakes in place. Glue the 7/8" FF stakes that are on the end to the upper side of the groove so that the Shaker tape can be inserted below it later.
3. Twine 1 rows with #2 round reed. Bend stakes up.
4. Weave 1 row of ½" FF reed making sure to go over the center stakes and then 3 rows of ¼" FF reed. Insert the ½" FO pieces over the four corner stakes, clip these together and weave as one stake.
5. Weave 1 row ½" FF reed
    1 row ¼" FF reed
    1 row ½" FF reed
    3 rows ¼" FF reed
    1 row 7/8" FF reed
    1 row ¼" FF reed
    1 row 7/8" FF reed
    3 row ¼" FF reed
    1 row ½" FF reed
    1 row ¼" FF reed
    1 row ½" FF reed
    3 row ¼" FF reed
    1 row ½" FF reed
    2 rows ¼" FF reed

   Note: Pull the weavers in slightly as you go up to give the basket a little shape.

6. Trim and tuck.
7. Use ½" FO for inner and out rims, fill with sea grass and double lash with ¼" FO reed.
8. After staining basket, insert the Shaker tape behind the ½" and 7/8" weavers on the end of the basket. Insert the ends in the groove under the 7/8" stake and glue in place.

Small Swing-Handle Tote Basket

Materials:
6" x 10" oblong wood base
11/64" FO reed
3/16" FF reed dyed black
¼" FF reed
7 mm FF reed
½" FF reed
½" FO reed
½" FF reed smoked
sea grass
CC handle package

Cutting:
Cut 32 stakes of ½" FF reed 9" long

Weaving:
1. Insert the 32 stakes evenly around the base.
2. Weave 1 row of 11/64" FO keeping the stakes flat and weaving inside the center stakes.
3. Gently upset the stakes and weave three more rows of 11/64" FO.
4. Weave the following rows flaring out slightly to make the top measure 9" x 13":
    7 rows ¼" FF
    2 rows 3/16" FF dyed black
    2 rows ¼' FF
    1 row ½" FF smoked
    2 rows ¼" FF
    2 rows 3/16" FF dyed black
    6 rows ¼" FF
    1 row 7 mm FF
5. Trim and tuck
6. Using ½" FO for inner and outer rims, fill with seagrass and double lash with 11/64" FO.
7. To attach handles, mark the rim above the stakes that are 2 away from the center stakes. (There are 3 stakes between the handle stakes.) Drill a hole through the rim above the four handle stakes. Insert screws as follows: screw, bead, handle, washer, rim & nut.

Hannah's Marriage Basket

Materials:
¼" FF reed
¼" FF reed smoked
3/8" FO reed
11/64" FO reed
#6 round reed
#10 round reed

Cutting:
Cut 12 pieces ¼" FF reed smoked 37" long
Cut 48 pieces ¼" FF reed smoked 27" long
Cut 2 pieces of #10 round reed 16" long

Weaving:
1. Mark centers of some pieces of each size.
2. Lay the 12 - 37" pieces horizontally on the table with the smooth side up since the bottom of the basket will be woven with the outside facing up.
3. Beginning 6 ¼" left of center with smooth side up, weave as follows:
    a) Stakes 1 & 2: O2, U4, O4, U2
    b) Stakes 3 & 4: U4, O4, U4
    c) Stakes 5 & 6: U2, O4, U4, O2
    d) Stakes 7 & 8: O4, U4, O4

   This sequence will be repeated 5 times across the bottom of the basket. When you are finished, turn the basket bottom over so that the smooth side is down.
4. Tie a piece of string around the horizontal stake on the edge between the 24th and 25th stakes. This is the center of the basket front.
5. Do not bend the stakes up. Gently roll them up and begin weaving right of center with ¼" natural reed weaving U3, O3 around the basket.
6. The first 6 rows are an O3-U3 twill pattern moving 2 stakes to the right on each row.
7. For rows 7 - 29, row by row instructions are given below. Start as indicated and repeat the portion around the basket.

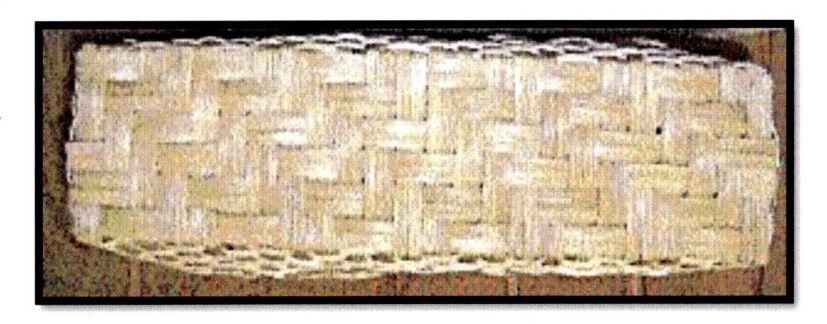

    Row 7: Begin at center, O3, U5, O3, U1.
    Row 8: Begin 3 stakes left of center, O5, U3, O1, U3.
    Row 9: Begin 2 stakes left of center, O3, U3.
    Row 10: Begin U3, O5, U3, O1.
    Row 11: Begin 3 left of center, U5, O3, U1, O3.
    Row 12: Begin 2 left of center, U3, O3.

Row 13: Begin 3 left of center, U5, O3, U3, O3, U1, O3, U3, O3.
Row 14: Begin at center, U3, O3, U3, O5, U3, O3, U3, O1.
Row 15: Begin 2 left of center, O3, U3.
Row 16: Begin 3 left of center, O5, U3, O3, U3, O1, U3, O3, U3.
Row 17: Begin at center, O3, U3, O3, U5, O3, U3, O3, U1.
Row 18: Begin 2 left of center, U3, O3.
Row 19: Repeat row 17.
Row 20: Repeat row 16.
Row 21: Repeat row 15.
Row 22: Repeat row 14.
Row 23: Repeat row 13.
Row 24: Repeat row 12.
Row 25: Repeat row 11.
Row 26: Repeat row 10.
Row 27: Repeat row 9.
Row 28: Repeat row 8.
Row 29: Repeat row 7.

8. Row 30: Begin 2 left of center and weave O3, U3.
9. Rows 31-36: Continue to weave a regular O3, U3 weave (not twill) pulling each group of 3 stakes together so that they can be treated as one.
10. Trim off the inside groups. Trim off 2 of the 3 stakes in the outside groups and tuck the remaining stake into the weaving.
11. Make handles as follows: Soak the 2 pieces of #10 round reed. Make marks 2" from each end and 2 ½" from each end. Notch it out between the markers about halfway through the depth of the reed. Taper the ends below the notches.
12. Use 3/8" FO reed for inner and outer rims and fill with #6 round reed. Insert handles between rims and insert ends under weavers. Cut #6 reed on each side of handles. Double lash with 11/64" FO reed.

Church Supper Basket

Materials:
10" x 16" rectangular wood base
#2 round reed
3/16" FO reed
¼" FO reed
½" FF reed
5/8" FF reed
5/8" FO reed
5/8" FF reed smoked
sea grass
10" round swing handles

Cutting:
Cut 44 stakes of 5/8" FF reed 6 ½" long

Weaving:
1. Insert the 44 stakes evenly around the base with 13 on the long sides and 9 on the short sides.
2. Twine 1 row of #2 round reed.
3. Gently bend stakes up and weave as follows:
    2 rows 3/16" FO reed
    4 rows ½" FF reed
    1 row 5/8" FF reed smoked
    3 rows ½" FF reed
4. Trim and tuck
5. Insert handles behind 5th stake from each corner on long sides.
6. Use 5/8" FF reed for inner rim, 5/8" FO reed for outer rim, fill with sea grass and lash with ¼" FO reed.

Small Twill Flag Tote

Materials;
4" X 8 ½" rectangular wood base
3/16" FO reed
1/4" FF reed
3/8" FF reed
3/8" FO reed
Sea grass
9" sq. oak handle
2" stoneware disc with flag

Cutting:
Cut from 3/8" FF reed 38 stakes 8" long

Weaving:
1. Insert 12 stakes on long sides of base, 5 stakes on short sides and 1 stake in each corner. Glue in place.
2. Tapering ends, weave 27 continuous rows of 3/16" FO reed in an over 2, under 1 twill pattern. Weave the first row with the stakes flat and then gentle bring them up to a vertical position in the next couple of rows.
3. Weave 1 row ¼" FF reed in twill pattern.
4. Insert handle.
5. Using 3/8" FO for both inner and outer rims, fill with sea grass and lash with 3/16" FO reed.
6. Attach flag disc.

Open Picnic Basket

Materials:
11" x 16" picnic basket base
2 – 12" swing handles
#3 round reed
3/16" FO reed
¼" FO reed
3/8" FF reed
½" FF reed
5/8" FF reed
5/8" FO reed
5/8" FF reed, dyed navy
5/8" FF reed, dyed red
Sea grass

Cutting:
Cut 44 stakes of 5/8" FF reed 13" long.

Weaving:
1. Insert 9 stakes on each end of base and 13 stakes on each side. Cut the corners off the end stakes on each side so that there is not a large gap in the corners.
2. Twine 1 row with #3 round reed.
3. Bend stakes up gently.
4. Weave 2 rows of 3/16" FO reed weaving 1st row outside the end stakes on the long sides on the first row.
5. Weave 12 rows of 3/8" FF reed.
6. Weave 1 row navy 5/8" FF reed, 1 row red 5/8" FF reed, 1 row navy 5/8" FF reed.
7. Weave 5 rows of 3/8" FF reed, 1 row ½" FF reed.
8. Trim and tuck.
9. Push handles down on 3rd or 4th stakes from ends on long sides.
10. Use 5/8" FF reed for inner rim and 5/8" FO for outer rim, fill with sea grass and lash with ¼" FO reed.

Braid and Twill Tote

Materials:
7 ½" x 10" rectangular wood base
#2 round reed
11/64" FO reed
3/16" FO reed
7mm FF reed
3/8" FF reed
½" FO reed
sea grass
10" square notched handle

Cutting:
Cut from 3/8" FF reed 52 stakes 9" long

Weaving:
1. Insert 15 stakes on long sides of base and 11 stakes on short sides. Trim corner stakes so they meet at corners.
2. Twine 1 row with #2 round reed.
3. Bend stakes up.
4. Continuous weave 6 rows of 7 mm FF reed in over 2, under 1 twill pattern tapering ends.
5. Taper the ends of 3 pieces of 3/16" FO reed (A, B, C) and weave 6 continuous rows of braid as follows:
    a) Begin with the three center spokes on a short side (1, 2, & 3) and place a weaver behind each one—A behind 1, B behind 2, and C behind 3.
    b) Take weaver A and go in front of spokes 2 and 3, under weaver C, behind 4 and out.
    c) Take weaver B and go in front of spokes 3 and 4, under the top weaver, behind 5 and out.
    d) The remainder of the braid continues this pattern which is similar to triple twining — take the left weaver, go over two spokes and under one but before going under one lift the upper weaver and go under it.
    e) Continue weaving the braid with these three weavers until 6 rows are completed. Taper ends above the original tapers.
6. Continuous weave 6 rows of 7 mm reed in twill as above.
7. Weave one row of 3/8" FF reed going over 1, under 1.
8. Trim and tuck.
9. Place handle so that the notch is even with the rim row inserting the tips under a couple of rows of weaving.
10. Use ½" FO for inner and outer rims, fill with sea grass and lash with 3/16" FO reed.

Chapter 11: Sectioned Baskets

Utensil Basket

Materials:
Utensil basket wood base
#2 round reed
¼" FF reed
5/8" FF reed
5/8" FF reed dyed
½" FF reed
½" FO reed
¼" FO reed
sea grass

Cutting:
Cut 28 stakes of 5/8" FF reed 7 ½" long

Weaving:
1. Insert the 28 stakes evenly around the base.
2. Twine 2 rows round reed
3. Weave 13 rows of ¼" FF reed. After the first row, begin lifting the stakes so that they are vertical after 5 or 6 rows.
4. Weave 1 row sea grass, 1 row 5/8" FF reed dyed, 1 row sea grass.
5. Weave 4 rows of ¼" FF reed.
6. Trim and tuck stakes.
7. Use ½" FF reed for inside rim and ½" FO reed for outside rim. Fill with sea grass.
8. Lash with ¼" FO reed.

Small Utensil Basket

Materials
Small utensil basket wood base
#2 round reed
3/16" FO reed
¼" FF reed
¼" FF reed dyed
3/8" FF reed
3/8" FO reed
5/8" FF reed
sea grass

Cutting
Cut 20 stakes of 5/8" FF reed 7" long

Weaving
1. Insert the 20 stakes evenly around the base.
2. Twine 2 rows of #2 round reed.
3. Weave 9 rows of ¼" FF reed. After the first row, begin lifting the stakes so that they are vertical after 5 or 6 rows.
4. Weave 1 row sea grass, 3 rows dyed 1/4" reed, 1 row sea grass.
5. Weave 3 rows of ¼" FF reed.
6. Trim and tuck stakes.
7. Use ½" FF reed for inside rim and ½" FO reed for outside rim. Fill with sea grass.
8. Lash with ¼" reed.

Desk Organizer Basket

Materials:
Desk organizer base
#2 round reed
¼" FF reed natural
¼" FF reed dyed
3/16" FO reed
½" FF reed
½" FO reed
sea grass

Cutting:
Cut 20 spokes of 5/8" FF reed 6" long

Weaving:
1. Insert the 20 spokes evenly around the base with one spoke at each divider.
2. Twine 2 rows of #2 round reed.
3. Weave 6 rows ¼" FF reed natural, 1 row sea grass, 1 row 5/8" FF dyed, 1 row sea grass, 4 rows ¼" FF.
4. Use ½" FF reed for inner rim and ½" FO reed for outer rim. Fill with sea grass.
5. Lash with ¼" FO reed.

Magazine Basket

Materials:
Magazine basket base
#2 round reed
3/16" FO reed
3/8" FF reed
½" FF reed
½" FO reed
5/8" FF reed
sea grass for filler
1 bundle braided sea grass

Cutting:
Cut 35 stakes of 5/8" FF reed 14" long

Weaving:
1. Insert the 35 – 5/8" stakes evenly around the base having one in the center at one end and one on each side of the center on the other end.
2. Weaving continuously, weave 4 rows of round reed.
3. Beginning between the two stakes on the divided end of the base, weave the braided sea grass in a continuous twill weave—over 2, under 1—almost to the top of the centerpiece of the base ending above where it began.
4. Tie the end of the braided sea grass to the row below with a piece of string.
5. Weave 1 row with 3/8" FF reed.
6. Trim and tuck.
7. Use ½" FF reed for inner rim and ½" FO reed for outer rim. Fill with sea grass.
8. Lash with 3/16" FO reed.

Twill Magazine Basket

Materials:
Magazine basket base
#2 round reed
¼" FF reed
½" FF reed
½" FF reed, smoked
5/8" FF reed
5/8" FO reed
sea grass for filler

Cutting:
Cut 35 pieces of 5/8" FF reed 14" long

Weaving:
1. Insert the 35 – 5/8" stakes evenly around the base having one in the center at one end and one on each side of the center on the other end.
2. Weaving continuously, weave 6 rows of round reed.
3. Bend stakes up.
4. Trim the last 4" of ½" FF smoked reed at an angle and beginning between the two stakes on the divided end of the base, weave the smoked reed in a continuous twill weave—over 2, under 1—almost to the top of the centerpiece (approx 19 rows).
5. Trim the last 4" of the smoked reed at an angle and end above where you began.
6. Weave 1 row for false rim with ½" FF reed continuing the twill pattern.
7. Trim and tuck.
8. Use 5/8" FF reed for inner rim and 5/8" FO reed for outer rim. Fill with sea grass.
9. Lash with 1/4" FF reed.

Large Magazine Basket

Materials:
10" x 13" rectangular base with 12" high divider and ball feet
3/16" FF reed
3/8" FF reed
#3 round reed
#6 round reed
½" FF reed smoked
5/8" FF reed
5/8" FO reed
¼" FO reed

Cutting:
Cut 44 stakes of 5/8" FF reed 13" long

Weaving:
1. Insert stakes in base—11 on long sides, 9 on short sides and 1 in each corner.
2. Twine 1 row w/#3 round reed.
3. Weave 2 rows 3/16" FO reed.
4. Weave 8 rows 3/8" FF reed.
5. Triple twine 1 row w/#3 round reed.
6. Continuous weave 7 rows w/1/2" FF smoked reed tapering ends and weaving 2x1 twill.
7. Triple twine 1 row w/#3 round reed.
1. Weave 7 rows 3/8" FF reed.
8. Trim and tuck.
9. Use 5/8" FO reed for inner and outer rims, fill with #6 round reed and lash with ¼" FO reed.

Short/Medium/Tall Divided Basket

Materials:
5" x 8" oval wood base with divider
#2 round reed
3/16" FO reed
¼" FF reed
½" FF reed smoked
½" FF reed
½" FO reed
5/8" FF reed
Sea grass

Cutting:
Cut 20 stakes of 5/8" FF reed 4 ½", (6 ½", 7 ½") long.

Weaving:
1. Insert stakes evenly in base.
2. Twine 2 rows with #2 round reed.

Short basket:
3. Weave 2 rows ¼" FF reed, 1 row ½" FF reed smoked, 6 rows ¼" FF reed.

Medium basket:
3. Weave 9 rows ¼" FF reed, 1 row ½" FF reed dyed, 6 rows ¼" FF reed.

Tall basket:
3. Weave 13 rows ¼" FF reed, 1 row sea grass, 1 row 5/8" FF reed, 1 row sea grass, rows ¼" FF reed.

4. Trim and tuck.
5. Use ½" FF reed for inner rim and ½" FO reed for outer rim, fill with sea grass and lash with ¼" FO reed.

Divided Craft Basket

Materials:
10" x 13" rectangular base with 10.5" high divider
3/16" FF reed
3/8" FF reed
#3 round reed
#6 round reed
5/8" FF reed, dyed red and navy
5/8" FF reed
5/8" FO reed
¼" FO reed

Cutting:
Cut 44 stakes of 5/8" FF reed 12" long
Cut 4 stakes of 5/8" FO reed 10" long

Weaving:
1. Insert stakes in base—11 on long sides, 9 on short sides and 1 in each corner.
2. Twine 1 row w/#3 round reed.
3. Weave 2 rows 3/16" FO reed weaving the first row outside the corner stakes.
4. Weave 15 rows 3/8" FF reed. After the third row push the 5/8" FO stakes into the weaving at the corners.
5. Weave 1 row red 5/8" FF reed, 1 row navy 5/8" FF reed and 1 row red 5/8" FF reed.
6. Weave 1 row 3/8" FF reed.
7. Trim and tuck.
8. Use 5/8" FF reed for inner rim and 5/8" FO reed for outer rim, fill with #6 round reed or sea grass and lash with ¼" FO reed.

Handy Caddy Basket

Materials:
Handy caddy wood base
#2 round reed
3/16" FO reed
3/8" FF reed
5/8" FF reed
5/8" FO reed
¼" FF or FO reed smoked
sea grass

Cutting:
Cut 32 stakes of 5/8" FF reed 7" long

Weaving:
1. Insert the 32 stakes into the base.
2. Weave two continuous rows of #2 round reed.
3. Bend stakes up.
4. Weave 7 rows of 3/8" FF reed, 1 row sea grass, 1 row 5/8" FF reed dyed, 1 row sea grass, then 2 more rows of 3/8" FF reed.
5. Trim and tuck.
6. Use 5/8" FF reed for inner rim, 5/8" FO reed for outer rim, fill with sea grass and lash with 3/16" FO reed.

Flat Caddy Basket

Materials:
Tableware caddy wood base
#2 round reed
3/16" FO reed
¼" FF or FO reed
3/8" FF reed
3/8" FO reed
½" FF reed, dyed
sea grass

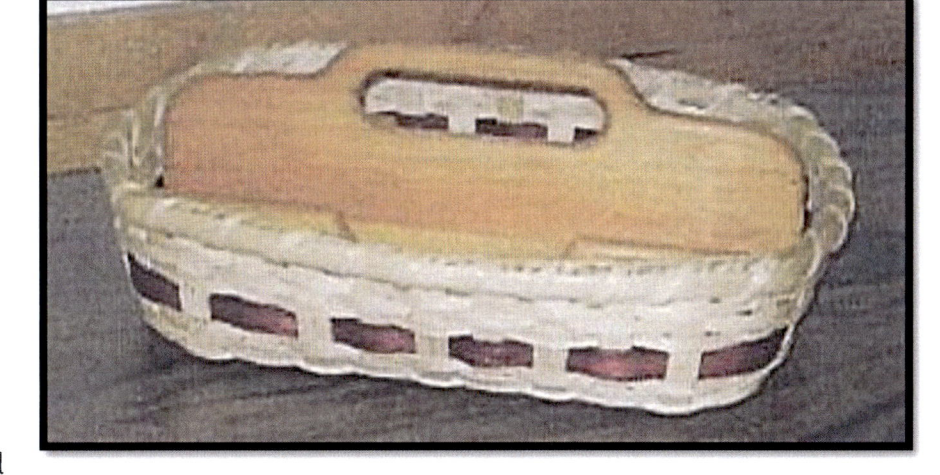

Cutting:
Cut 28 stakes of 5/8" FF reed 5" long

Weaving:
1. Insert stakes in base with 7 on each side, 5 on each end and 1 in each corner.
2. Twine 3 rows with #2 round reed.
3. Gently bend stakes up and weave 2 rows ¼" FF or FO reed, 1 row ½" FF dyed reed, and 6 rows ¼" FF reed. (If using FO, weave 5 rows FO and 1 row FF.)
4. Trim and tuck.
5. Use 3/8" FF reed for inner rim and 3/8" FO reed for outer rim. Fill with sea grass.
6. Lash with 3/16" FO reed

Sarah's Basket

Materials:
11" x 13" rectangular wood base
#2 round reed
3/16" FO reed
1/4" FF reed
1/2" FF reed
1/2" FO reed
sea grass

Cutting:
Cut 24 stakes of 1/2" FF reed 10" long

Weaving:
1. Insert stakes evenly in base.
2. Twine 2 rows with #2 round reed.
3. Weave ? rows.
4. Weave a false rim row of 3/8"FF
5. Trim and tuck.
6. Use 1/2" FF reed for inner rim, 1/2" FO for outer rim and sea grass for filler.
7. Double lash with 3/16" FO reed.

Weaver's Workbasket

Materials
Weaver's workbasket base
#2 round reed
3/16" FO reed
¼" FF reed
¼" FF reed, dyed
3/8" FF reed
3/8" FO reed
1/2" FF reed
sea grass
4 decorative furniture nails

Cutting
Cut 40 stakes of ½" FF reed 5 ½" long

Weaving
1. Insert stakes into base placing one stake on each side of each partition, nine stakes between partitions and nine stakes around ends.
2. Chase weave or twine 2 rows with #2 round reed.
3. Bend stakes up gently.
4. Weave 8 rows 1/4" FF reed, 1 row 5/8" dyed reed and 3 rows 1/4" reed.
5. Trim and tuck.
6. Use 3/8" FF reed for inner rim, 3/8" FO reed for outer rim and fill with sea grass.
7. Lash with 3/16" FO reed.
8. Tack the sides to the upright partitions.

Tool Basket

Materials
Tool basket wood base
#2 round reed
¼" FF reed
¼" FF reed dyed
5/8" FF reed
5/8" FO reed
3/16" FO reed
sea grass

Cutting
Cut 40 pieces of 5/8" FF reed 8" long

Weaving
1. Insert the 40 stakes evenly around the base. Place 1 at the end of each partition, 5 between partitions, and 13 around each end.
2. Chase weave 2 rows round reed
3. Weave 13 rows of ¼" FF reed. After the first row, begin lifting the stakes so that they are vertical after 5 or 6 rows.
4. Weave 5 rows of dyed ¼" FF reed.
5. Weave 4 rows of ¼" FF reed.
6. Trim and tuck stakes.
7. Use 5/8" FF reed for inside rim and 5/8" FO reed for outside rim. Fill with sea grass.
8. Lash with 3/16" FO reed.

Peanut Basket

Materials:
12 ½" peanut base with handle
#2 round reed
¼" FF reed
¼" FF reed dyed
¼" FO reed
3/8" FF reed
½" FF reed
½" FF reed dyed
½" FO reed
5/8" FF reed
Sea grass

Cutting:
Cut 36 stakes of 5/8" FF reed 7" long

Weaving:
1. Insert stakes evenly in base.
2. Twine 1 row w/#2 round reed.
3. Bend stakes up.
4. Weave 1 row 3/8" FF reed weaving outside the stakes by the handle, 3 rows ¼" reed, 2 rows dyed ¼" reed, 2 rows ¼" reed, 1 row ½" dyed reed, 2 rows ¼" reed, 2 rows dyed ¼" reed, 3 rows ¼" reed, 1 row 3/8" reed.
5. Trim and tuck.
6. Use ½" FF reed for inner rim and ½" FO reed for outer rims, fill with sea grass and lash with ¼" FO reed.

Jelly Jar Basket

Materials:
Jelly jar wood base, 3" x 7" base with 6 ½" high handle, ½" wood
#2 round reed
3/16" FO reed
¼" FF reed
½" FF reed
½" FF reed dyed
½" FO reed
Sea grass

Cutting:
Cut 20 stakes of ½" FF reed 4 ½" long

Weaving:
1. Insert the 20 stakes evenly in the base.
2. Twine 1 rows with #2 round reed.
3. Bend stakes up.
4. Weave 4 rows of ¼" FF reed, 1 row ½" FF reed dyed, 5 rows ¼" FF reed.
5. Trim and tuck.
6. Use ½" FF for inner rim, ½" FO for outer rim, fill with sea grass and lash with 3/16" FO reed.

Picnic Caddy Basket

Materials:
Picnic caddy wood base
#2 round reed
3/16" FO reed
¼" FO reed
¼" FF reed dyed
3/8" FF reed
½" FF reed
½" FF reed dyed
½" FO reed
5/8" FF reed
5/8" FO reed
Sea grass

Cutting:
Cut 22 stakes of 5/8' FF reed 7" long
Cut 6 stakes of ½" FF reed 7" long
Cut 4 pieces of 5/8" FO reed 5" long

Weaving:
1. Insert stakes in base—one 5/8" FF in each corner, seven 5/8" FF on the long sides and on the short sides insert one 5/8", three ½" and one 5/8".
2. Twine 1 row with #2 round reed.
3. Weave 2 rows of 3/16" FO reed weaving the first row outside the corners.
4. Weave 6 rows 3/8" FF. After the third row insert the 5/8" FO pieces vertically in the corners.
5. Weave 1 row ½" FF reed dyed, 1 row ¼" FF reed dyed, 1 row ½" FF reed dyed, and 2 rows 3/8" FF reed.
6. Trim and tuck
7. Use ½" FO reed for outer rim, ½" FF reed for inner rim, fill with sea grass and lash with ¼" FO
8. Use small tacks to fasten rim to all partitions.

Chapter 12:
For the Holidays

Easter Basket

Materials:
4"x6" rectangular wood base
#2 round reed
1/4" FF reed
1/4" FO reed
1/2" FF reed
5/8" FF reed
7/8" FF reed
1" FF reed
1/4" FF reed dyed
1/2" FF reed dyed
1 strip of fabric 2"x36" (bias preferably)

Cutting:
14 stakes 1/2" FF reed 9" long, 4 natural and 10 dyed (assorted colors)
2 stakes 7/8" FF reed 8" long
4 stakes 1" FF reed 8" long
2 pieces 7/8" FF reed 23" long for handle

Weaving:
1. Insert 7/8" stakes in center of short sides of base.
2. Insert 1" stakes in corners of base. (Trim corners slightly.)
3. Insert 10 dyed stakes in base--5 on each long side and insert 1 natural stake on each short side between the 7/8" stake and the 1" stake.
4. Chase weave twice around with #2 round reed. (4 rows of reed.)
5. Cut the 1" corner pieces in thirds lengthwise and spread the pieces apart so that you can weave between them.
6. Chase weave 3 more rounds. (10 rows altogether.)
7. Chase weave 4 more rounds gently lifting the sides so that there is about a 45 degree angle after 18 rows.
8. Weave 9 rows 1/4" FO reed. Weave loosely so that the side flare out a little.
9. Leave a 1" gap for fabric (3 clothespins) and weave the next row same as last row.
10. After 3 rows remove clothespins and make sure gap is 1".
11. Weave 2 more rows of 1/4" FO (5 rows altogether above gap).
12. Weave 1 row 1/2" FF reed for false rim.
13. Trim and tuck.
14. Bend the ends of one of the handle pieces under 1/2" and push under false rim lining up with the 7/8" stakes.
15. Use 5/8" FF reed for both inner and outer rims and fill with sea grass.
16. Lash with 1/4" FF reed.
17. Lay the other handle piece under the first piece and lay a piece of 1/4" FF reed dyed on top of the handle and wrap handle with 1/4" FF reed going over and under the 1/4" piece.

Stars and Stripes Basket

Materials:
4 1/2" round wood base
3/16" FO reed
3/8" FF reed
1/2" FF reed
1/4" FF reed dyed red
1/4" FF reed dyed navy
#2 round reed
sea grass
stars painted white

Cutting:
Cut 16 pieces of 1/2" FF reed 8" long

Weaving:
1. Insert the 16 stakes into the base.
2. Weave 4 rows of #2 round reed.
3. Bend stakes up.
4. Weave 9 rows beginning with 3/8" FF reed and alternating with 1/4" red reed.
5. Weave 5 rows 1/4" FF navy reed.
6. Weave 1 row 3/8" FF reed for false rim.
7. Trim and tuck.
8. Use 1/2" FF reed for both inner and outer rims. Fill with sea grass.
9. Lash with 3/16" FO reed
10. Glue stars on every other stake.

Stars and Stripes Basket with Handle

Materials:
5" round wood base
1/4" FF reed
3/8" FF reed
1/2" FF reed
1/4" FF reed dyed red
1/4" FF reed dyed blue
#2 round reed
sea grass
stars painted white

Cutting:
Cut 14 stakes of 1/2" FF reed 8" long
Cut 2 stakes of 5/8" FF reed 8" long

Weaving:
1. Insert the 16 stakes into the base with the 5/8" pieces on opposite side.
2. Weave 4 rows of #2 round reed.
3. Bend stakes up.
4. Weave 9 rows beginning with 3/8" FF reed and alternating with 1/4" red reed.
5. Weave 5 rows 1/4" FF blue reed.
6. Weave 1 row 3/8" FF reed for false rim.
7. Trim and tuck.
8. Use 1/2" FF reed for both inner and outer rims. Fill with sea grass.
9. Insert ends of 5/8" stakes in opposite sides to form handle.
10. Lash with 3/16" FO reed.
11. Wrap handle with 1/4" FF reed.
12. Glue stars on every other stake.

Christmas Basket #1

Materials:
5" x 8 ½" oval wood base
#2 round reed
3/16" FO reed
¼" FF reed
¼" FO reed
½" FF reed
5/8" FF reed
5/8" FO reed
7/8" FF reed
sea grass
Christmas fabric—3 ¼" x 36"

Cutting:
Cut 22 stakes of ½" FF reed 7" long
Cut 2 handle stakes of 7/8" FF reed 28" long
Cut 1 handle piece of 7/8" reed 24" long

Weaving:

1. Insert the two 7/8" FF reed handle stakes in the ends of the base and insert 11 of the ½" FF stakes on each side.
2. Twine one row with #2 round reed. DO NOT CUT!
3. Add a third strand of #2 round reed and triple twine 4 rows lifting sides.
4. Weave 7 rows of ¼" FO reed lifting sides but keeping them slanting outward.
5. Leave a 1 1/8" gap (3 clothespins) and weave 3 rows of ¼" FO reed weaving the first of these rows the same as the row before the gap.
6. Weave 1 row ½" FF reed.
7. Trim and tuck.
8. Push ends of handle into edges trimming to desired length. Add the third piece of 7/8" FF reed inside handle.
9. Use 5/8" FF for inner rim and 5/8" FO for outer rim. Fill with sea grass and lash with 3/16" FO reed.
10. Wrap handle with ¼" FF reed wrapping around a piece of ¼" FF natural or dyed reed.
11. Fold the fabric lengthwise with right sides together, sew a narrow seam, turn so that right side is out and weave through the gap left in the basket.

Christmas Basket #2

Materials:
10" Square ash handle w/dip
3/16" FO reed
3/8" FF reed
½" FF reed
5/8" FF reed
5/8" FF reed dyed
5/8" FO reed
7/8" FF reed
#2 round reed
Fiber rush
Pottery ornament

Cutting:
Cut 1 stake of 7/8" FF reed 26" long
Cut 4 stakes of ½" FF reed 26" long
Cut 9 stakes of ½" FF reed 22" long
Cut 4 fillers of 3/8" FF reed 16" long

Weaving:
1. Mark centers of stakes and fillers.
2. Lay the 7/8" stake horizontally on the table.
3. Lay the ½" FF on each side above and below.
4. Lay the fillers horizontally between the stakes.
5. Weave a 24" stake vertically at center weaving under the long stakes and over the fillers.
6. Weave the remaining stakes on each side of center. Push long stakes tight together — 4 ½" x 9 ½".
7. Bend fillers to inside and tuck.
8. With #2 round reed, start at a corner and twine 1 row. DO NOT CUT.
9. Bend stakes up and twine 5 more rows.
10. Weave 1 row of dyed reed weaving over 7/8" stakes.
11. Weave 12 rows of 3/8" FF reed.
12. Trim and tuck.
13. Insert handle.
14. Using 5/8" FF reed for inner rim and outer rim, fill with fiber rush and lash with 3/16" reed.
15. Tie on pottery ornament.

Santa Basket

Materials:
5" x 8 ½" oval wood base
#2 round reed
11/64" FO reed
¼" FF reed
¼" FF reed dyed red
3/8" FF reed
3/8" FF reed dyed red
½" FF reed
5/8" FF reed
Sea grass
2 – ¾" black buttons for eyes
1 – 5/8" red button for nose

Cutting:
Cut 22 stakes of ½" FF reed 10" long
Cut 2 stakes of 5/8" FF reed 22" long

Weaving:
1. Insert stakes evenly in base with the 5/8" stakes on the ends.
2. Twine 2 rows of #2 round reed.
3. Bend stakes up.
4. Weave 1 row of 3/8" FF reed weaving outside the end stakes. Weave 16 additional rows of 3/8" FF for a total of 17 rows. Keep all ends on the back of the basket so they don't interfere with the beard.
5. Trim and tuck.
6. Fold handles over and tuck ends in to make handle double. Add a third piece of 5/8" reed to make handle stronger.
7. Use ½" FF reed for inner and outer rims and seagrass for filler. Lash with 11/64" FO reed.
8. Wrap handle with ¼" FF reed.
9. Make beard:
    a) Starting on row 3 of the basket, tuck the end of the ¼" FF reed under the stake that is left of the center stake. Make a loop and tuck the other end under the stake to the right of the center stake.
    b) On row 4, insert the ¼" FF end under the stake to the left of the previous one, make a loop, slide the piece under the center stake, make a loop and insert end under the next stake on the right.
    c) On row 5, move one stake to the left and repeat the above procedure making 3 loops.
    d) Repeat this procedure on rows 6 and 7 making 4 and then 5 loops.
    e) On the row 8, repeat the procedure from row 6.
    f) On the next three rows, the beard is split. On row 9, start under the 5th stake left of center and make 2 loops ending under the stake to the left of center. Begin the other side under the stake to the right of center, make two loops ending behind the 5th stake right of center.
    g) On row 10, begin under the 4th stake left of center and make one loop. In the other side begin under the 2nd stake right of center and make one loop.

- h) In row 11, begin under the 5th stake left of center and make two loops. On the right, start under the 2nd stake right if center and make one loop.
- i) On row 12 there are 4 loops. Begin under the 4th stake left of center and end under the 4th stake right of center. Make the 2nd and 3rd loops very small to allow space for the eyes.
- j) On row 13 there will be 3 loops. Begin under the 3rd stake left of center and end under the 3rd stake right of center.

10. Make hat:
    - a) Insert one end of a strip of 3/8" FF reed dyed red under the 2nd stake left of center and the other end under the handle.
    - b) Insert a 2nd piece of red reed under the 1st stake left of center with the other end under the 1st stake behind the handle.
    - c) Insert a piece of red reed under the center stake with the other end behind the handle.
    - d) Cut 5 pieces of 3/16"FF reed dyed red in graduated lengths from 11" to 15". Insert these pieces under the right side of the red rows and insert the opposite ends under the weaver on the 13th row over the 5th stake from center. Glue in place.

11. Glue buttons in place for eyes and nose.

Chapter 13: Using Hoops

Melon Basket

Materials:
Two 8" rings glued together at a 90-degree angle
¼" FF reed
#6 round reed

Cutting:
Cut 6 primary ribs of #6 round reed 12 ½" long
Cut 4 secondary ribs of #6 round reed 11" long
With a sharp knife, make a point on the ends of all ribs.

Weaving:
1. Soak 2 pieces of ¼" FF reed at least 8' long several minutes until very pliable.
2. Weave God's eye as follows:
   - With smooth side out, place the end of the ¼" reed where the dot is in the diagram.
   - Move diagonally up and around (1).
   - Then move diagonally down to (2).
   - Go up around (2) and then diagonally down to (3).
   - Go behind (3) and then diagonally up to (4).
   - Go down behind 4 and then repeat (b) - (f) until there are 6 revolutions counting from the back. Make sure that the god's eye is very flat. Do NOT cut the reed.
3. Secure the end with a clothespin and repeat God's eye on the other side.
4. Insert 3 ribs into the God's eye on each side of the handle.
5. Remove clothespin and begin weaving over and under the ribs and the handle.
The rows of reed should be pushed snugly against each other but do not pull too tight when weaving as the ribs will be distorted.
6. After 4 complete rows, add the secondary ribs between the primary ribs.
7. Continue the over-under weaving pattern. Weave a few rows on one side and then a few rows on the other side until the two sides meet in the middle. Push the weavers out from the center to complete the last few rows, if necessary.

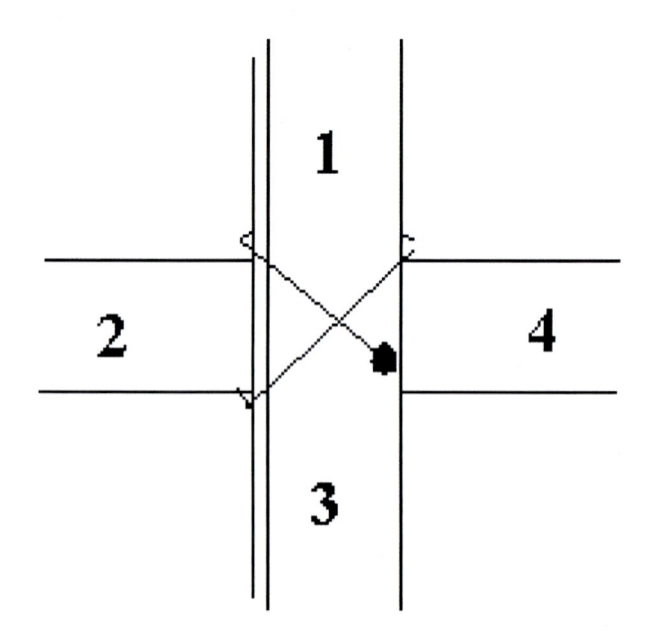

Cat Head Basket

Materials:
11/64" FO reed
¼" FF reed
3/8" FF reed
½" FF reed
½" FO reed
¼" FF reed, navy
½" FF reed, burgundy
sea grass
8" hoop

Cutting:
Cut 16 stakes of 3/8" FF reed 20" long
Cut 2 stakes of ½" FF reed 20" long
Cut 1 handle of ½" FO reed 19" long

Weaving:
1. Mark centers of all stakes on rough side.
2. Lay 9 stakes vertically on the table with a ½" stake in center and four 3/8" stakes on each side. With the other ½" stake in the center, weave the remaining stakes horizontally to form a 5 ½" x 5 ½" square.
3. Bend stakes up.
4. Weave 2 rows with ¼" FF reed.
5. Divide the 8" hoop into quarters and mark. Using clothes pins, fasten the marked points to the ½" center stakes about 1" above the weavers.
6. Continue weaving with ¼" FF reed using the hoop as a mold.
7. Weave 14 rows altogether moving the hoop up as needed.
8. Weave 1 row of ¼" FF navy, 1 row of ½" FF burgundy, 1 row of ¼" FF navy, 3 rows of ¼" FF natural, and 1 false rim row of 3/8" FF natural.
9. Trim and tuck. Do not tuck ½" stakes. Cut them off even with the top edge.
10. Make a cut across the handle piece ¾" from each end on the curved side. Shave off curve for about ½" above the cut to create a ledge. Shave off end below ledge and carve sides to form a blunt point.
11. Use ½" FO for inner and outer rims and fill with sea grass.
12. Push handle down between false rim and inner rim on a pair of opposite sides so that the ledge catches on the false rim.
13. Lash with 11/64" FO reed.

Potato Basket

Materials:
8" round wood hoop
#6 round reed
¼" FF reed

Cutting:
Cut ribs of round reed as follows:

3 primary ribs - 17"	Secondary ribs--
2 A ribs - 11 ½"	2 a ribs - 11 ½"
2 B ribs - 13 "	2 b ribs - 13"
2 C ribs - 14 ½"	2 c ribs - 13 ½"
2 D ribs - 15"	2 d ribs - 14"

Weaving:
1. Divide circumference of hoop in half and make pencil marks. Make marks 1" away on each side of these points. Then make marks at the quarter points of the hoop.
2. On the outside of each of the 3 primary ribs, cut a notch ¼" from each end. Below the notch, scoop out an area half the thickness of the rib and as long as the width of the hoop.
3. Tie one of the ribs at both halfway points on the hoop. Tie another rib on each of the 1" marks beside the halfway points.
4. With a long piece of ¼" FF reed, make X's on top of the three primary ribs as shown in the diagram above.
5. After making X's, go over K, under L, over M, around the rim. Continue weaving in this manner making a flat area between the rim and the last rib until you have gone 6 times around the rim on both sides. Do this on both sides of the basket. DO NOT CUT WEAVERS.
6. Sharpen ends of all remaining primary ribs (A,B,C,D). Insert the A ribs into the opening just below the rim. Insert the B ribs into the same opening just below the A ribs. With an awl, create an opening in the flat area of the lashing and insert the C ribs. Insert the D ribs in the opening between the C ribs and the primary ribs.
7. Measure 2" on each side of the remaining marks on the rim and mark 4" spaces for handles.
8. Continue weaving over and under the ribs and around the rim until you have woven 5 rows on each side.
9. Insert secondary ribs in the same opening as primary ribs--a with A, b with B, etc.
10. Continue weaving over and under. When you reach the marks for the handles, stop weaving the rim and turn around on the top rib. When this space fills up, turn around on a lower rib. Weave until all space is filled in.
11. Wrap handle, if desired.

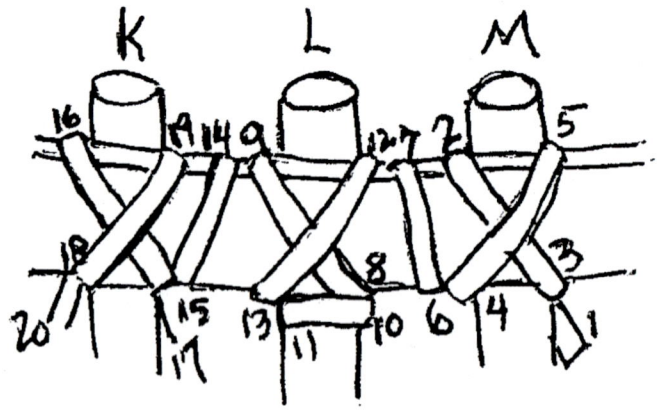

Melon Basket with Yarn

Materials:
2 – 8" round hoops
11/64" FF reed
¼" FF reed
#6 round reed
Bulky yarn

Cutting:
Cut 6 primary ribs of #6 round reed 12 ½" long
Cut 4 secondary ribs of #6 round reed 11" long

Weaving:
1. Soak 2 pieces of ¼" FF reed at least 8' long several minutes until very pliable.
2. Weave God's eye as follows:
    a) With smooth side out, place the end of the ¼" reed where the dot is in the diagram.
    b) Move diagonally up and around (1). Then move diagonally down to (2).
    c) Go up around (2) and then diagonally down to (3).
    d) Go behind (3) and then diagonally up to (4).
    e) Go down behind 4 and then repeat (b) - (f) until there are 6 revolutions counting from the back. Make sure that the god's eye is very flat. Tuck the end under the weaving.
3. Repeat God's eye on the other side.
4. Insert 3 primary ribs into the God's eye on each side of the handle.
5. With 11/64" FF reed, begin weaving over and under the ribs and the handle. Weave four rows on each side.
6. With yarn weave 8 – 10 rows or as desired.
7. Add the secondary ribs between the primary ribs.
8. Continue the over-under weaving pattern with ¼" FF reed. The rows of reed should be pushed snugly against each other but do not pull too tight as the ribs will be distorted.
9. Weave a few rows on one side and then a few rows on the other side until the two sides meet in the middle. Push the weavers out from the center to complete the last few rows, if necessary.

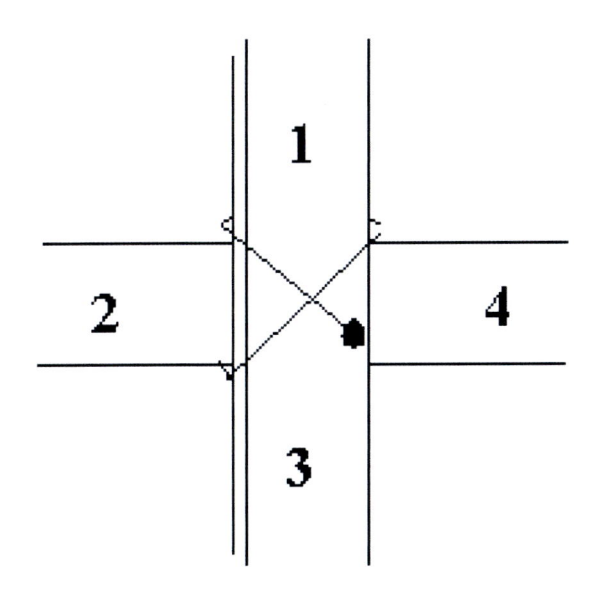

Chapter 14: Decorative Weaving

Diamond Weave Basket

Materials:
¼" FF reed natural
¼" FF reed dyed
3/8" FF reed
½" FF reed natural
½" FF reed dyed
sea grass
 raffia or waxed cotton thread

Cutting:
Cut 18 pieces of ½" FF reed 22" long

Weaving:
1. Lay 5 stakes vertically on the table with a 6" spread from right to left.
2. Weave the remaining stakes tightly together as follows:
   - Weave the first stake over, under, over, under, over.
   - Weave the second stake exactly the same.
   - Weave the third and fourth stakes opposite of the first two.
   - Weave the fifth and sixth stakes the same as the first two.
   - Weave the seventh stake the same as the third and fourth.
   - Weave the remaining 6 stakes the same as the first 6.
3. Check the bottom to see that it measures 6" x 7".
4. Bend all stakes up. The 5 stakes will be the sides of the basket and the 11 will be front and back.
5. All weaving will be done with ½" FF dyed reed until otherwise noted. Start all weaving on the sides weaving over, under, etc. and weave the front and back as follows:
   - Row 1 – Under 2, over 2, under 2, over 1, under 2, over 2, under 2.
   - Row 2 – Over 3, under 2, over 3, under 2, over 3.
   - Row 3 – Over 2, under 2, over 2, under 1, over 2, under 2, over 2.
   - Row 4 – Over 1, under 2, over 2, under 3, over 2, under 2, over 1.
   - Row 5 – Under 2, over 2, under 2, over 1, under 2, over 2, under 2.
   - Row 6 – same as 4.
   - Row 7 – same as 3.
   - Row 8 – same as 2.
   - Row 9 – same as 1.
6. Weave 1 row of 3/8" FF weaving over-under on sides and whatever works on front and back.
7. Trim and tuck.
8. Use ½" FF for both inside rim and outside rim. Fill with sea grass.
9. Cut a 36" piece of ½" FF reed for handle. At the center of each side, push the handle under the top row of dyed reed and the outer rim. Bring the ends together at the center so that the handle is double.
10. Lash rim with raffia or waxed thread in a needle.
11. Wrap handle with ¼" FF reed laying in a row of dyed ¼" FF reed dyed.

Whitecaps Basket

Materials:
6" round wood base
#3 round reed
#4 round reed
#6 round reed
1/4" FF reed, space dyed

Cutting:
Cut 25 spokes of #4 round reed 17" long

Weaving:
1. Insert the spokes into the groove of the base spacing them evenly.
2. Mark spoke 1.
3. Weave a twined arrow as follows:
   a) Twine one row with #3 (4') round reed ending with the weavers coming from behind spokes Y and Z.
   b) Do a twining step-up: Bring the right weaver in front of one spoke, behind one spoke and out. Repeat with the left weaver.
   c) Work a row of reverse twining: Lift the right weaver, with the left weaver go in front of one spoke, behind one spoke and out. Repeat around until spokes are coming out behind Y and Z.
   d) End the arrow by bring the left weaver under spoke 1 and threading the other weaver under the top weaver and ending behind spoke 2.
4. Pinch the spokes and then push them up gently.
5. Work a locked four-rod coil:
   a) Insert four pieces of #4 round reed behind spokes 1, 2, 3 and 4.
   b) Bring the left weaver in front of three spokes and out. Repeat until the spokes are coming from behind W, X, Y and Z.
   c) Work the step-up and lock: Bring the right weaver in front of three spokes and behind the next spoke. Repeat with remaining weavers. Trim ends.
6. Weave three rows of three-rod wale working a step-up at the end of each row. Cut ends.
7. Work 9 rows of basic wave weave as follows:
   a) Taper the end of a piece of 1/4" FF reed for about 3" and place it behind spoke 1, place a piece of #3 round reed behind spoke 2 below the flat weaver.
   b) With the flat weaver rand twice, then weave the round reed behind spoke 4 above the flat reed.
   c) Bring the round reed diagonally down in front of spoke 5 and behind spoke 6 below the flat weaver.
   d) Continue randing the flat weaver with the round reed weaving above and below it.
   e) At the end of the 9th row, taper the flat reed and cut off the round reed.

8. Work two rows of three-rod wale with a step-up at the end of each row.
9. Prepare border core of #6 round reed by carving both ends so that they fit smoothly together.
10. Work the Japanese rolled border variation 1 around the core as follows:
    a) Place the core outside the spokes, bring each spoke in front of three spokes and in underneath the core.
    b) Work a row of over two and down.
    c) Repeat the above step.
    d) Trim the spokes.

Wave Basket

Materials:
4 ½" round wood base
¼" FF reed, dyed or space-dyed
3/8" FF reed
#3 round reed
#4 round reed

Cutting:
Cut 25 spokes of #4 round reed 15" long

Weaving:
1. Insert the spokes evenly in the groove of the base.
2. Mark spoke 1.
3. Twine 2 rows with #3 round reed. Do not cut.
4. Pinch the spokes and bend them up.
5. Add a third piece of #3 round reed and triple twine 4 rows.
6. Work 12 rows of basic wave weave as follows:
    a) Taper the end of a piece of 1/4" FF reed for about 3" and place it behind spoke 1, place a piece of #3 round reed behind spoke 2 below the flat weaver.
    b) With the flat weaver rand twice, then weave the round reed behind spoke 4 above the flat reed.
    c) Bring the round reed diagonally down in front of spoke 5 and behind spoke 6 below the flat weaver.
    d) Continue randing the flat weaver with the round reed weaving above and below it.
    e) At the end of the 12th row, taper the flat reed and cut off the round reed.
7. Triple twine 2 rows with #3 round reed.
8. Weave the edge as follows (make sure that the spokes are very wet.):
    a) Bring any spoke behind the one to the right and down.
    b) Push the end of each spoke into the loop at the right.
    c) Go one over one and down on the inside.
    d) Repeat above step.
    e) When dry, cut off long ends.

Japanese Diamond Bowl

Materials:
5.5" round wood base (1/2" thick)
    with 26 horizontal holes (7/64")
#2 round reed
#3 round reed
#4 round reed
¼" FF reed dyed

Cutting:
Cut from #4 round reed 26 spokes
    21" long
Cut from #4 round reed 4 pieces
    23" long for four-rod coil.

Weaving:
1. Insert the 26 spokes into the holes around the base.
2. Work a locked four-rod coil around the base:
    a) Turn the base upside down and with 4 pieces of #4 round reed, work a 4-rod locked coil:
    b) Insert a #4 round reed weaver behind spoke #1 and the next 3 spokes.
    c) Bring the left spoke in front of three spokes, behind one and out. Continue to spoke #1.
    d) Work a step-up--bring the right weaver in front of 3 spokes and behind one. Lift the original weaver and go under it and out to lock the coil. Repeat with 3, 2 and 1.
    e) Turn over and tighten the coil by pulling ends in opposite directions. Trim ends.
3. Pinch the spokes to bend up.
4. Twine 2 rows with #3 round reed doing a step-up between the rows.
5. Weave 6 continuous rows of Japanese weave as follows:
    a) Prepare two pieces of #2 round reed and one piece of ¼" dyed FF reed tapering the last 5" of the FF reed.
    b) Select three consecutive #4 round stakes. Place the end of a #2 round reed behind the 2nd stake. Above it, place the tapered end of the FF reed behind the 1st stake, weave it in front of the 2nd stake, behind the 3rd stake and out. Above that, place the end of the other #2 round reed behind the 2nd stake. We will refer to these three weavers as x, y and z. The upper round weaver will be called x, the FF weaver will be y and the lower round weaver will be z.
    c) Bring x diagonally down in front of stake #3, go under weaver y and behind stake #4 and out.
    d) Weave y in front of stake #4, behind stake #5 and out.
    e) Weave z up over stake #3, behind stake #4 and out.
    f) Continue steps c thru e around the basket 6 times ending with a taper above the initial taper.
6. Twine 3 rows with #3 round reed doing step-eps.
7. Work a basic rolled border:
    a) Behind two and out
    b) In front of three and in
    c) Over two and down
    d) Over two and down
8. Trim ends of stakes.

Oval Basket with Japanese Diamond Weave

Materials:
7" x 11" oval wood base with 35 holes
¼" FF reed
¼" FO reed, dyed dark brown
#2 round reed
#3 round reed, dyed dark brown
#4 round reed

Cutting:
Cut 35 stakes of #4 round reed 21" long

Weaving:
All round reed must be well-soaked before weaving.

1. Insert the #4 round stakes into the holes in the base. Leave 3 5/8" extending below the base and weave as follows:
    a) When 5 stakes have been inserted, take the first stake behind the second stake (toward the center of the basket), then in front of the third and fourth stakes and behind the fifth stake.
    b) As each new stake is inserted into its hole, repeat the above weaving sequence.
2. Weave three continuous rows of ¼" FF reed tapering the ends. Pull out as you are weaving so that the basket will flare out slightly.
3. Triple twine one row with #3 dyed round reed.
4. Weave three continuous rows of Japanese diamond weave as follows:
    a) Prepare two pieces of #2 round reed and one piece of ¼" dyed FO reed approx. 3 ½ yards long. Taper the last 5" of the FO reed.
    b) Select three consecutive #4 round stakes. Place the end of a #2 round reed behind the 2nd stake. Above it, place the tapered end of the FO reed behind the 1st stake, weave it in front of the 2nd stake, behind the 3rd stake and out. Above that, place the end of the other #2 round reed behind the 2nd stake. We will refer to these three weavers as x, y and z. The upper round weaver will always be called x, the FO weaver will be y and the lower round weaver will be z.
    c) Bring x diagonally down in front of stake #3, go under weaver y and behind stake #4 and out.
    d) Weave y in front of stake #4, behind stake #5 and out.

- e) Weave 7 up over stake #3, behind stake #4 and out.
- f) Continue steps c thru e around the basket 3 times.
5. Repeat step 3.
6. Repeat step 2.
7. Re-wet the stakes and work a basic rolled border:
    - a) With needle-nose pliers, bend each stake just above the weaving. Going right, take each stake behind 2 and out.
    - b) Bring each stake over three stakes that are sticking out, go in under the loops formed by the 1st row.
    - c) Working inside the basket, go over two and down.
    - d) Repeat the last step.
    - e) Push rows tightly together. Trim ends so that a ½" end remains.

Urn Basket

Materials:
6" wood base
#2 round reed
#2 round smoked reed
#3 round reed
1/4" FO reed
1/4" FO smoked reed
3/8" FF reed
1/2" FO reed
#0 sea grass
#1 sea grass
#2 sea grass

Cutting:
Cut 29 pieces 1/2" FF reed 12" long
Cut 29 pieces 1/2" FO reed 7 ½" long

Weaving:
1. Insert the 1/2" pieces into wood base.
2. Weave 4 rows #2 round. DO NOT CUT.
3. Bend stakes up.
4. Add 2 pieces #2 round reed and triple weave 6 rows.
5. Twine 2 rows with #2 smoked reed.
    Note: There will generally be 2 rows of twining after each woven section of pattern. Be sure to measure from the table to the top of the twining at various intervals after each twining to make sure that the distances are equal. If they are not equal, adjust the weaving so that the basket does not become lopsided.
6. Triple weave 7 rows using 2 strands of #3 round reed and 1 strand #0 sea grass (5 1/2 yards).
7. Repeat step 5.
8. Diagonal weave the 29 pieces of 1/4" FO reed.
9. Repeat step 5.
10. Insert the end of a 4-yard piece of #1 sea grass between two stakes. Insert the end of a piece of #2 round reed between the next two stakes and bring it around the sea grass and behind the next stake and out to the front. Keeping the sea grass in front of the stakes, continue wrapping the round reed around it for four rows.
11. Repeat step 5.
11. Triple weave 7 rows with 3 strands of #3 round reed.
12. Weave 3 continuous rows of 1/4" smoked reed.
13. Twine 8 rows of #3 round reed.
14. Weave a false rim using 3/8" FF reed.
15. Cut inside stakes even with false rim. Bend outside stakes, cut them even with bottom edge of false rim.
16. Use 1/2" FO reed for inner and outer rims, fill with sea grass and lash with 3/16" FO reed.

Braided Urn Basket

Materials:
7" round wood base
#3 round reed dyed
½" FF reed smoked

Cutting:
Cut 24 stakes of ½" FF reed smoked 13" long
Cut 72 pieces of ½" FF reed for braiding 9" long
Cut 24 pieces of #3 round reed 10" long

Weaving:
2. Insert the 24 stakes evenly around the base and glue in place.
3. Turn upside-down and twine 1 row with #3 round reed and do a step-up.
4. Turn over and twine 6 more rows lifting stakes slightly. Do a step-up at the end of each row.
5. Mark every other stake 1¼" and 1½" above the last row of twining. Mark these stakes twice more 1¼" and 1½" above the last mark. Then mark stakes 1¼" above last mark.
6. Twine two rows between the first pair of marks making a diameter of approx. 9".
7. Twine two rows between the second pair of marks making a diameter of approx. 10".
8. Twine two rows between the third pair of marks making a diameter of approx. 10".
9. At the last set of marks twine 8 rows pulling in to a diameter of about 7" at the top.
10. Soak the spokes. Trim and tuck under several rows of twining.
11. Soak the 72 - ½" FF braid pieces. Insert a piece behind a stake just below the 8 rows of twining with the smooth side facing the inside of the basket. Bring the ends together and cross the left side over the right. Tuck the right end under the double row of twining. Trim the left end if necessary and tuck it under the double row of twining.
12. Make two more braids below the first one.
13. Repeat this procedure around the basket.
14. Insert a piece of well-soaked #3 round reed into the twining beside a stake at the top of the basket. Repeat this around the basket.
15. Make a braided edge around the top of the basket by following these steps:
    a) Starting anyplace, bring a piece of reed behind the piece to the right and down to the outside. Repeat this around the basket.
    b) Take any piece and insert it in the loop to the right and inside.
    c) Go one over one and down on the inside.
    d) Repeat the above step.
    e) When dry, cut ends.

Ridge-Weave Basket

Materials:
7" round wood base (1/2" thick)
    with 26 horizontal holes (3/32")
#2 round reed dyed black
#3 round reed
#4 round reed
#4 round reed smoked
3/8" FF reed

Cutting:
Cut from #4 round reed 26 spokes
    20" long
Cut from #4 round reed smoked 26
    spokes 20" long

Weaving:
1. Insert the 26 spokes into the holes around the base.
2. Work a four-rod coil around the base.
3. Pinch the spokes and bend them up.
4. Weave 6 rows of three-rod wale shaping the sides slightly outward.
5. Add dyed side spokes into pockets between spokes.
6. Weave 6 rows of ridge weave using #2 round reed dyed and 3/8" FF reed. Taper the ends of the 3/8" FF reed and chase weave continuously weaving the 3/8" FF reed over the original spokes and under the dyed spokes.
7. Pinch the spokes so they bend inward and work 8 rows of three-rod wale incorporating the added dyed spokes.*
    *To incorporate the added dyed spokes, the three ends of the pieces of round reed must be placed behind three consecutive dyed spokes. (Mark the first of these spokes.) Bring the left weaver in front of three spokes, behind three spokes and out. Do a step-up each time you get to the marked spoke.
8. First border: Pinch the dyed spokes and work a rolled border —
    a) Behind 2 and out.
    b) Over 2 and down on the outside.
    c) Repeat b.
    d) Repeat b again.
9. Second border:
    a) Bring each undyed spoke over the top to the outside, in front of 3 dyed spokes to the right, then to the inside just above the 5th row of three-rod wale.
    b) Work 2 rows of over 2 and down on the inside.

Diamondback Basket

Materials:
8" round wood base
11/64" FO reed
3/16" FO reed
#2 round reed
¼" reed, dyed dark brown
3/8" FF reed
½" FO reed
Sea grass

Cutting:
Cut 64 stakes of ¼" FF reed dyed 10" long

Weaving:
1. Insert the 64 stakes evenly around the base.
2. Mark every 16th stake at the top end.
3. Taper the last 4" of a piece of 3/16" FO reed and weaving over 2, under 1 weave 7 rows. Bring this up very gradually weaving it to a diameter of about 10".
4. Triple twine 1 row with #3 round reed.
5. Weave diamond pattern starting at one of the marked stakes and rotating basket each row to begin at a different marked stake. Leave an inch or two free at the beginning of each row and work it into the pattern at the end of the row. The pattern will repeat four times around the basket. Each time you get to a marked stake you will be back at the beginning.
    1) u1, o1, u1, o4, u2, (o1, u1) 3x, o1.
    2) o1, u1, (o2, u2) 2x, (o1, u1) 3x.
    3) u1, o2, u2, o1, u1, o2, u2, (o1, u1) 2x, o1.
    4) o2, u2, (o1, u1) 2x, o2, u2, (o1, u1) 2x.
    5) Back up 1 stake from the marked stake and go o2, u2, (o1, u1) 3x, o2, u2, o1, u1.
    6) u2, (o1, u1) 4x, o2, u2, o2.
    7) Back up 1 stake from the marked stake and go u2, (o1, u1) 5x, o4.
    8) Repeat step 6.

162

9) Repeat step 5.
10) Repeat step 4.
11) Repeat step 3.
12) Repeat step 2.
13) Repeat step 1.
6. Triple twine 1 row with #3 round reed.
7. Weave 12 rows going over 2, under 2 pulling in on each row so that the top is approx. 7" in diameter.
8. Weave 1 row of ¼" FF reed for false rim
9. Trim as follows: cut off inner stakes; cut off one of each pair of the outer stakes and trim the other to about 1/2" and bend it down.
10. Use ½" FO for inner and outer rims, fill with sea grass and lash with 11/64" FO reed.

Diagonal Weave Basket

Materials:
½" FF reed
½" FF reed, smoked
#1 round reed
#5 round reed

Cutting:
Cut 16 pieces ½" FF reed natural 34" long
Cut 4 pieces ½" FF reed smoked 34" long

Weaving:
1. Mark centers of ½" FF smoked pieces and lay 2 of them horizontally on the table. Lay 4 pieces of ½" FF natural reed on each side of them.
2. Weave the verticals following the chart placing the two smoked reed pieces in the center. Base must measure 6"x6".
3. Twine once around the base with #1 round reed.
4. Pick up base, fold two adjacent corners up so that a corner forms between two of the smoked reeds with all of the stakes on the left crossing those on the right. Begin weaving these reeds together as follows:
    a) Weave the left smoked reed over 2, under 2.
    b) Weave the right smoked reed under 2, over 2.
    c) The 1st natural reed on the left is over the smoked reed but after that it goes under 2, over 2.
    d) The 1st natural reed on the right is under the smoked reed but after that it goes over 2, under 2.
    e) The 2nd natural reed on the left is under 2 so then weave it over 2.
    f) The 2nd natural reed on the right is over 2 so then weave it under 2.
    g) The 3rd natural reed on the left is under 1, weave it over 2.
    h) The 3rd natural reed on the right is over 1, weave it under 2.
    i) The 4th natural reed on the left is over 2, weave it under 2.
    j) The 4th natural reed on the right is under 2, weave it over 2.
5. Repeat step 4 at each of the corners.
6. Continue weaving all stakes under 2, over 2.
7. Cut top off evenly at desired height.
8. Use ½" reed for inner and outer rims, fill with #5 round reed and lash with #1 round reed.

U	U	O	O	U	O	U	U	O	O
U	O	O	U	U	O	O	U	U	O
O	O	U	U	O	U	O	O	U	U
O	U	U	O	O	U	U	O	O	U
U	U	O	O	O	U	U	U	O	O
O	O	U	U	U	O	O	O	U	U
U	O	O	U	U	O	O	U	U	O
U	U	O	O	U	O	U	U	O	O
O	U	U	O	O	U	U	O	O	U
O	O	U	U	O	U	O	O	U	U

Zigzag Basket

Materials:
6" round wood base
#0 round reed
11/64" FO reed
3/16" FO reed
¼" FF reed, dyed
¼" FO reed
3/8" FF reed
½" FF reed
½" FO reed
Cane (2.75 mm)
Sea grass

Cutting:
Cut 50 spokes of ¼" FF reed 9 ½" long

Weaving:
1. Without soaking, insert spokes evenly around base and glue in place.
2. Using 3/16" FO reed, weave one row weaving under 3, over 2 pulling tight so that the spokes begin to lift.
3. Weaving from the outside of the basket, move 1 spoke to the left with pattern, gently bend spokes up and weave 1 row with ¼" FO reed.
4. Continue weaving with ¼" FO reed moving 1 spoke to the left each row until there are 10 rows woven including the row of 3/16" FO reed.
5. Continue moving 1 spoke the left each row and weave 2 rows 3/16" FO reed, 2 rows 11/64" FO reed and 1 row of cane using the back (non-shiny) side of the cane.
6. Moving to the right 1 stake on each r, weave 2 rows 11/64" FO reed, 2 rows 3/16" FO reed and 9 rows ¼" FO reed.
7. Continuing the pattern, weave 1 row 3/8" FO reed.
8. Trim and tuck.
9. Use ½" FF reed for inner rim, ½" FO reed for outer rim, fill with sea grass and lash with 3/16" FO reed.

Flying Geese Basket

Materials:
5" x 8" oval base
#2 round reed
3/16" FO reed
1/4" FF reed
3/8" FF reed
1/2" FF reed
1/2" FO reed
1/4" FF reed, dyed
sea grass

Cutting:
Cut 28 stakes ½" FF reed 9 1/2" long
Cut 2 handles 3/8" FF reed 14" long

Weaving:
1. Insert the 28 - 1/2" stakes into the base.
2. Chase weave 2 rows #2 round reed.
3. Bend stakes up.
4. Weave 4 rows 3/8" FF reed.
5. Weave flying geese pattern as follows:
    - Weave 1 row 1/4" dyed reed weaving over two stakes and then under two stakes.
    - Weave next row the same but start one stake to the right of the previous row.
    - Continue above step until 6 rows of dyed reed are woven.
    - Weave next five rows the same but move one stake to the left before starting each row.
6. Weave 5 rows 3/8" FF reed.
7. Trim and tuck.
8. Insert each handle under false rim on opposite sides of basket. Insert ends of each piece about 3" apart and bend so handles are double thickness of reed.
9. Use 1/2" FF reed for inner rim and 1/2" FO reed for outer rim. Fill with sea grass.
10. Lash with 3/16" FO reed.
11. Wrap handles with 1/4" FF reed.

Snow-Capped Mountains Basket

Materials:
8" rounded square base
11/64" FO reed
3/16" FF reed dyed black
7 mm FF reed
#5 round reed
½" FO reed

Cutting:
Cut 96 stakes of 7 mm FF reed 9" long

Weaving:
1. Insert one stake in each corner of base and 23 stakes on each side.
2. Weave pattern according to the chart on the next page. The top row is the false rim row and should be woven with 7 mm, undyed reed.
3. Trim and tuck. Tuck every 6th stake selecting the ones that do not interrupt the pattern.
4. Using ½" FO reed for inner and outer rims, fill with #5 reed and lash with 11/64" FO reed.

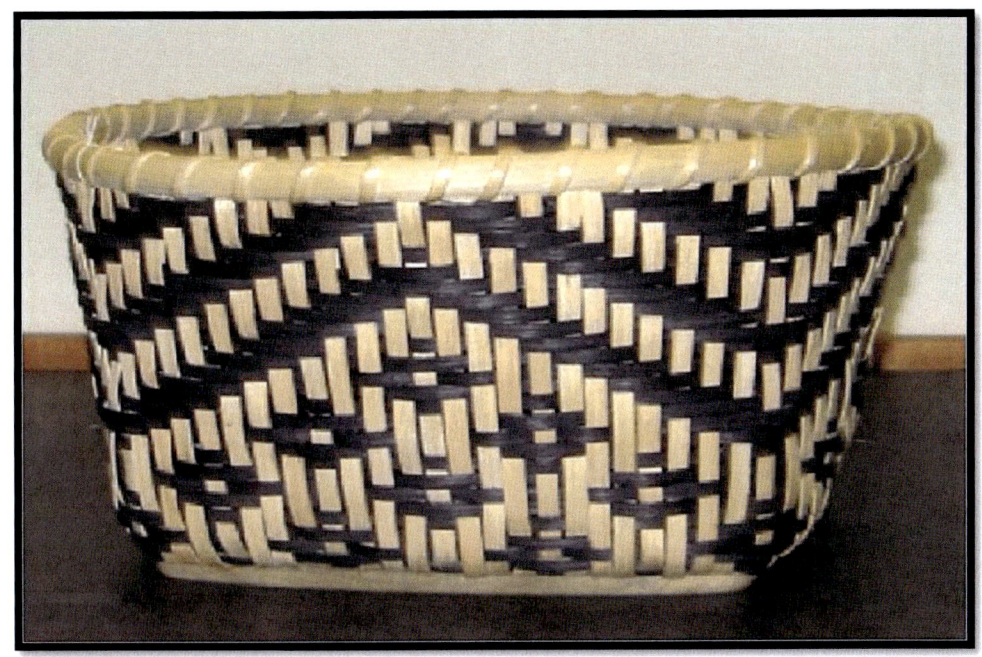

Row	1	2	3	4	5	6	7	8	9	10	11	12	13	14	15	16	17	18	19	20	21
27	O				O	O	O			O	O	O	O	O			O	O	O			O
26			X	X	X			X	X	X		X	X	X			X	X	X			
25		X	X	X			X	X	X				X	X	X			X	X	X		
24		X	X	X		X	X	X						X	X	X			X	X	X	
23	X	X	X			X	X	X			X			X	X	X				X	X	X
22	X	X			X	X	X			X	X	X			X	X	X				X	X
21	X			X	X	X			X	X	X	X	X			X	X	X				X
20			X	X	X			X	X	X		X	X	X			X	X	X			
19		X	X	X			X	X	X				X	X	X			X	X	X		
18		X	X	X		X	X	X						X	X	X			X	X	X	
17	X	X	X			X	X	X			X			X	X	X				X	X	X
16	X	X			X	X	X			X	X	X			X	X	X				X	X
15	X			X	X	X			X	X		X	X			X	X	X				X
14			X	X	X					X	X	X					X	X	X			
13		X	X	X			X			X			X				X	X	X			
12		X	X	X		X	X	X					X	X	X			X	X	X		
11	X	X	X			X		X	X			X		X	X				X	X	X	
10	X	X				X	X	X			X	X	X							X	X	
9	X			X			X			X			X			X						X
8			X	X	X				X	X	X					X	X	X				
7		X	X		X	X			X	X		X	X			X	X		X	X		
6			X	X	X				X	X	X					X	X	X				
5	X			X		X			X			X			X			X				X
4	X	X				X	X	X					X	X	X						X	X
3		X	X			X	X		X	X		X	X		X	X				X	X	
2	X	X				X	X	X					X	X	X						X	X
1	X			X			X			X			X			X				X		X

|corner |center   corner|

Bird Nest Basket

Materials:
5" round wood base
#2 round reed
3/8" FF reed

Cutting:
Cut 20 stakes of 3/8" FF reed 8 ½" long
Cut 100 pieces of #2 round reed 5" long

Weaving:
1. Insert stakes evenly in base with smooth sides up.
2. Twine 1 row with #2 round reed, turn base over, bend stakes up gently and twine another row. Do not cut.
3. Add a third strand of #2 round reed and triple twine 9 rows with step-ups. Keep the sides coming straight up so that the diameter is 5".
4. Soak 20 of the 5"-pieces and bend them so they curved at the center. Lay one behind each stake so that the bend is behind the stake. Triple twine 1 row.
5. Repeat the last step until there are five rows of the "nest" pieces.
6. Continue triple twining until there are 8 rows above the "nest".
7. Cut off one strand and twine four rows with 2 strands of #2 round reed.
8. Cut a piece of 3/8" FF reed to fit around the top of the basket and clip it inside the stakes just above the last row of twining.
9. Finish with a check-mark edge as follows:
    a) Soak the tops of the stakes again so that they are very bendable.
    b) Start with one stake, fold it over the rim and bring it out in the space between it and the next stake.
    c) Bend it up so that it crosses over the next stake and cut it off so that it is hidden behind the third stake.
    d) Repeat the above procedure around the basket.

Little Drummer Boy Basket

Materials
5" round wood base
#2 round reed
3/16" FO reed
3/16" FF reed, navy
¼" FF reed
¼" FF reed, red
3/8" FF reed
5/8" FF reed
3/4" FF reed
3/4" FF reed, navy
sea grass

Cutting
Cut 18 stakes of 5/8" FF reed 10" long
Cut 2 handle stakes of 3/4" FF reed 26" long

Weaving
1. Trim off the corners of the 2 handle stakes of 3/4" FF reed and insert them in opposite sides of base.
2. Insert 9 of the remaining stakes on each side of the base.
3. Chase weave with #2 round reed to a diameter of 7" ending with a row that goes over the handles.
4. Bend stakes up.
5. Weave I row navy 3/4" reed.
6. Weave 1 row red 1/4" reed.
7. With 3/16" FO reed, double lash the navy row making an "X" in each navy block.
8. Continue weaving alternating 1 row 3/8" FF reed with 1 row 1/4" FF red reed until there are 13 rows beginning and ending with red.
9. Weave 1 row 5/8" FF reed for false rim.
10. Trim and tuck.
11. Use 3/4" FF navy reed for both inner and outer rims and fill with sea grass.
12. Push handle ends between the rim rows on opposite sides.
13. Double lash with 3/16" FO reed so that the "X's" line up with the "X's" on the bottom.
14. Wrap handle with 1/4" FF reed (12').
15. Cut 20 pieces of 3/16" FF navy reed 5 1/2" long and inset them around basket under navy rims as shown in picture above.

Blueberry Bucket

Materials:
8" round wood base
10" swing handle
#2 round reed
¼" FO reed
¼" FF reed
¼" FF reed, dyed
½" FF reed
5/8" FF reed
5/8" FF reed, dyed
5/8" FO reed
sea grass

Cutting:
Cut 14 stakes of 5/8" FF dyed reed 10" long
Cut 14 stakes of ½" FF reed 10" long

Weaving:
1. Insert dyed and natural stakes alternately in base.
2. Twine 1 row with #2 round reed.
3. Weave 14 rows of ¼" FF reed weaving over dyed 5/8" stakes on first row and bringing to a diameter of 10" by the 10th row.
4. Weave 2 rows dyed ¼" FF reed, 1 row 5/8" FF reed, 2 rows dyed ¼" reed.
5. Weave 7 rows ¼" FF reed.
6. Weave a false rim of ½" FF reed.
7. Trim and tuck.
8. Insert handle.
9. Use 5/8" FO reed for inner and outer rims and fill with sea grass.
10. Lash with ¼" FO reed.

Spiral Basket

Materials:
5" round base
3/16" FO reed
3/16" FO reed, smoked
¼" FF reed
3/8" FO reed
#6 round reed

Cutting:
Cut 40 stakes of ¼" FF reed 6" long

Weaving:
1. Insert the stakes in the base with smooth sides up and glue in place.
2. Weave 18 continuous rows of over 2, under 1 twill with 3/16" FO smoked reed with a taper at both ends. Keep the weaving fairly flat for the first four rows and then curve up gradually.
3. Weave 1 row of ¼" FF reed weaving in pattern.
4. Trim all outside stakes and tuck all inside stakes to the outside.
5. Use 3/8" FO reed for inner and outer borders, fill with #6 round reed and lash with 3/16" FO reed.

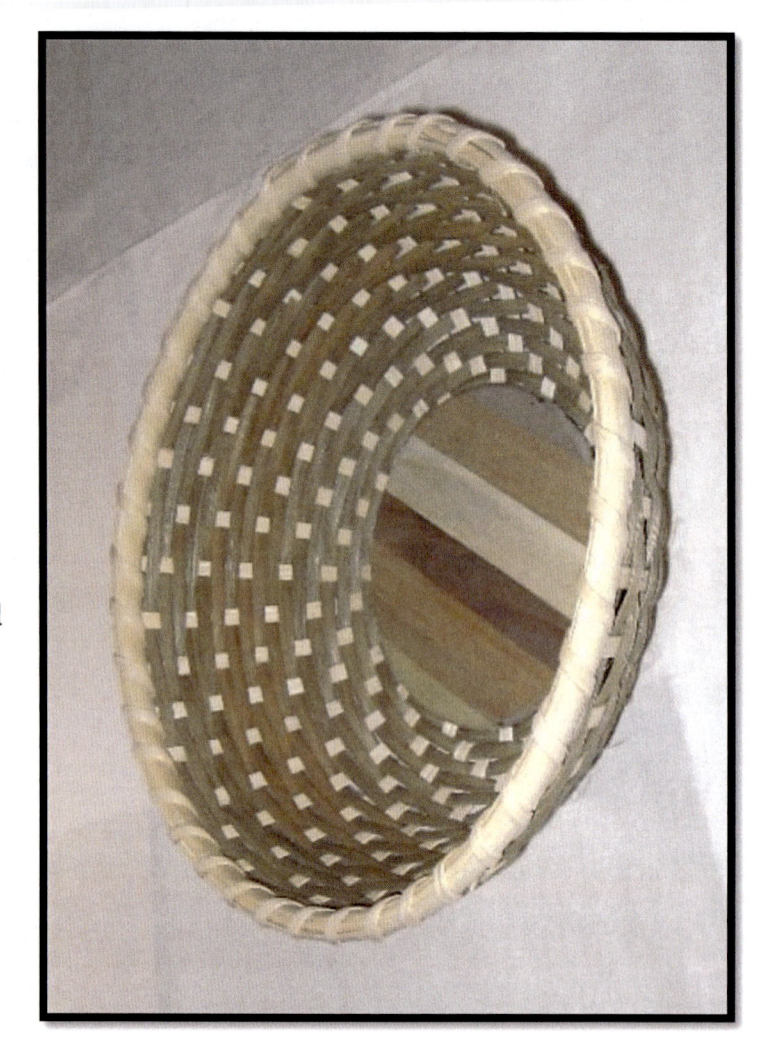

Star Swirl Basket

Materials:
11/64" FO reed
3/16" FO reed
¼" FF reed
¼" FF reed, dyed
3/8" FF reed
3/8" FO reed
#5 round reed

Cutting:
Cut 14 stakes of ¼" FF reed 19" long
Cut 28 stakes of ¼" FF reed, dyed 19" long

Weaving
Weave this basket with the smooth sides up. Before beginning, lightly mark the centers of two of the dyed stakes.

1. Lay 4 natural stakes, 1 dyed marked stake and 4 natural stakes horizontally on the table.
2. Weave the other dyed marked stake vertically under the center of the center horizontal stake.
3. Weave a natural stake vertically on each side going under 3 stakes in the center.
4. Weave a natural stake vertically on each side going under 5 stakes in the center.
5. Weave a natural stake vertically on each side going under 7 stakes in the center.
6. Weave a dyed stake vertically on each side going under 4, over 1, under 4.
7. Weave a dyed stake horizontally above and below going under 4, over 1, under 4.
8. The remainder of the base weaving will be done with the dyed stakes continuing the above sequence as follows:
    a) vert—u4, o3, u4
    b) horiz—u4, o3, u4
    c) vert—u4, o5, u4
    d) horiz—u4, o5, u4
    e) vert—u4, o7, u4
    f) horiz—u4, o7, u4
    g) vert—u4, o4, u1, o4, u4
    h) horiz—u4, o4, u1, o4, u4
    i) vert—u4, o4, u3, o4, u4
    j) horiz—u4, o4, u3, o4, u4
    k) vert—u4, o4, u5, o4, u4
9. Taper the last 5" of a long piece of 3/16" FO reed.
10. Bring the ends of the two stakes at each corner up and clip them together.

11. Begin weave with the 3/16" FO piece at one of the corners by going under 2, over 3 leaving at least a 1" tail of the tapered end extending beyond the first stake in the corner. Continue weaving under 2, over 3. This is a continuous weave so keep going. For the first few rows pull fairly tightly around the corners. After the first few rows, go loosely around the corners and begin to spread the stakes so that the corners are filled in and the stakes are somewhat evenly distributed. Continue to spread the stakes so that by the 9th or 10th row they form a circle.
12. After 18 rows of weaving, gently bend the stakes upward and weave 1 more row. On this row, the stakes and the weaver should be pointing straight up. Taper the last 4" of the weaver so that the tapered end is above the starting taper.
13. Weave 1 row of ¼" FF reed for false rim.
14. Trim and tuck. Tuck every 5th stake to the inside using the stakes that do not interrupt the pattern. Do the same on the outside.
15. Use 3/8" FF for inner rim, 3/8" FO for outer rim, fill with #5 round reed and lash with 11/64" FO reed.

Amish Tray

Materials:
¼" reed dyed four colors
3/8" FF or FO reed
Waxed thread

Cutting:
Cut 68 stakes of ¼" reed 18" long
   14 – color 1 (burgundy)
   18 – color 2 (blue)
   16 – color 3 (green)
   20 – color 4 (smoked)

Weaving:
Since the inside of the basket is what will be seen, all weaving will be done with the smooth side up.

1. Lay 7 burgundy stakes horizontally side by side.
2. Weave 1 burgundy piece vertically under the center of the center piece.
3. Weave a piece of burgundy on each side of the first piece going under the center 3 pieces.
4. Weave 2 more pieces beside the others going under 5 pieces.
5. Weave the last 2 pieces under all 7 pieces.
6. Weave a piece of blue horizontally above and below the burgundy pieces going under all 7 pieces.
7. The next 2 pieces of blue will be woven vertically on each side of the burgundy pieces going under 4, over 1 and under 4.
8. The next two pieces of blue will be woven the same as above but horizontally.

9. Continue weaving alternating vertical and horizontal and always going under or over 4 except for the burgundy center which will be either over or under 1, 3, 5 or 7 in that order. When all 18 blue stakes are used, begin with green and then follow with smoked.
10. To weave the sides, locate a center stake on any side. On each side of the center stake is an "over 4". With a long piece of smoked weaver, move one stake to the right of the above "over 4" and create a new "over 4". Continue weaving over 4, under 4 all the way around the basket making a bend at the corners. Weave 7 rows altogether moving 1 stake to the right on each row.
11. Trim and tuck. All tucking will be done to the outside. It is only necessary to tuck one of every 6 or 8 stakes. Tuck any stake that has a place on the outside where it can be conveniently tucked. Trim off all remaining stakes making sure that they are even with the top edge but not below it.
12. Use 3/8" FF or FO for inner and outer rims and sea grass for filler. Lash with waxed thread.

Chapter 15: Misc. Baskets

Kettle Basket

Materials:
¼" FF reed
3/16" FO reed
3/8" FF reed
½" FF reed
½" FO reed
5/8" FF reed
round reed
sea grass
8" wire handle
4 – 1" wooden ball feet

Cutting:
Cut 10 pieces of 5/8" FF reed 23" long

Weaving:
1. Mark centers of the 10 cut pieces on wrong side. Lay 5 stakes horizontally with wrong sides up and weave the remaining 5 stakes vertically so that the base is 5 1/4" x 5 1/4".
2. Bend stakes to inside.
3. Weave 2 rows of 3/8" FF reed. DO NOT BREAK CORNERS.
4. Begin weaving with ¼" FF reed. After 5 rows begin to flare sides. Weave 10 rows of ¼" FF altogether.
5. Weave 8 rows with 3/8" FF reed weaving straight up after reaching a diameter of 8".
6. Trim and tuck stakes.
7. Hook handle under center weavers on the second row down.
8. Use ½" FF reed on inside rim, ½" FO on outside and fill with sea grass.
9. Lash with 3/16" FO reed.
10. Attach wooden ball feet to bottom corners.

Kettle Basket with Wood Base

Materials:
5.25" x 5.25" wood base w/1" ball feet attached
8" wire handle
#2 round reed
3/16" FO reed
¼" FF reed
3/8" FF reed
½" FF reed
½' FO reed
Sea grass

Cutting:
Cut 20 stakes of 5/8" FF reed 9.5" long

Weaving:
1. Insert stakes in groove of base, 5 on each side.
2. Twine 1 row of #2 round reed.
3. Bend stakes up.
4. Weave 2 rows of 3/8" reed. DO NOT BREAK CORNERS.
5. Weave with ¼" FF reed. After 5 rows begin to flare sides. Weave 10 rows of ¼" FF altogether.
6. Weave 8 rows with 3/8" FF reed weaving straight up after reaching a diameter of 8".
7. Trim and tuck stakes.
8. Hook handle under center weavers on the second row down.
9. Use ½" FF reed on inside rim, ½" FO on outside and fill with sea grass.
10. Lash with 3/16" FO reed.

Small Oval Basket with Wire Handle

Materials:
4" x 6" oval wood base
mini bean pot handle w/eyelets
#2 round reed
3/16" FO reed
¼" FF or FO reed natural
¼" FF reed dyed
3/8" FF reed
3/8" FO reed
½" FF reed
sea grass

Cutting:
Cut 20 pieces of ½" FF reed 7" long

Weaving:
1. Insert the 20 spokes evenly around the base making sure that there are 2 center spokes for handle placement.
2. Continuous weave 4 rows around the base with round reed starting the weaving over a center spoke.
3. Weave 1 row of ¼" FF or FO reed keeping spokes flat.
4. Begin raising spokes and weave 4 additional rows ¼" FF or FO reed.
5. Keeping basket size to 5" x 8", weave 1 row ¼" FF reed dyed, 1 row natural, 3 rows dyed, 1 row natural, 1 row dyed, 4 rows natural.
6. Trim and tuck spokes placing eyelets at center spokes and catching them under the tucking.
7. Use 3/8" FF for inner rim and 3/8" FO for outer rim. Fill with sea grass.
8. Lash with 3/16" FO reed.
9. Attach handle to eyelets.
10. Add decorative design with #2 round reed if desired.

Oval Twill Basket with Wrought Iron Handle

Materials:
8"x10" oval wood base
¼" FF reed
3/8" FF reed
5/8" FO reed
11/64" FO reed
#1 round reed
Sea grass
8" wrought iron round top handle with spiral

Cutting:
Cut 41 stakes of 3/8" FF reed 9" long

Weaving:
1. Insert the 41 stakes evenly around the wood base.
2. Twine 2 rows with #1 round reed.
3. Begin continuous weave as follows:
    a) Taper the last 4" of ¼" reed.
    b) Weave an over 2, under 2 twill.
4. Weave 23 rows ending with a taper above the initial taper.
5. Twine 2 rows with #1 round reed.
6. Trim and tuck, tucking all ends.
7. Insert handle ends under the tucking.
8. Use 5/8" FO reed for inner and outer rims, fill with sea grass and lash with 11/64" FO reed.

Large Oval Basket with Wire Handle

Materials:
6"x11" oblong wood bottom
#2 round reed
¼" FF reed
¼" FO reed
¼" FF reed, dyed
½" FF reed
5/8" FF reed, smoked
5/8" FO reed
Sea grass
Eyelet
8" x 8" wire handle

Cutting:
Cut 32 stakes of 5/8" FF reed 9" long

Weaving:
1. Insert the stakes evenly in the base.
2. Twine 5 rows around base doing a step-up at the end of each row flaring to a measure of 7" x 12".
3. Weave as follows bringing basket to a dimension of 10" x 14":
    a) 4 rows ¼" FF reed going outside the center stakes on the first row.
    b) 2 rows ¼: FF reed, dyed
    c) 2 rows ¼" FF reed
    d) 1 row 5/8" FF reed, smoked
    e) 2 rows ¼" FF reed
    f) 2 rows ¼" FF reed, dyed
    g) 5 rows ¼" FF reed
    h) 1 row ½" FF reed
4. Trim and tuck placing the two eyelets in the centers of the sides and tucking the ends under the stakes on each side of center.
5. Use 5/8" FO for inner and outer rims, fill with sea grass and lash with ¼" FO reed. When lashing, go through the eyelets.
6. Attach handle to eyelets.

Ribbon Basket

Materials:
6" square wood base
#3 round reed
#4 round reed
#8 round reed
11/64" FO reed
3/16" FO reed
3/8" FO reed
½" FF reed

Cutting:
Cut 26 stakes of ½" FF reed 6 ½" long
Cut 2 pieces of ½" FF reed 21" long for handle stakes
Cut 1 piece of ½" FF reed 18" long for handle filler

Weaving:
1. Insert 7 stakes on each side of base with handle stakes centered on opp. sides.
2. Twine once around base with #3 round reed.
3. Bend stakes up.
4. Weave 11 rows of 3/16" FO reed weaving under handle stakes. Do not break corners. Pull in slightly so that the circumference after 11 rows is 23".
5. Push handle ends down into weaving on opp. sides. Insert handle filler between handle stakes. Handle should be about 7 ¼" above base.
6. Using pieces of 1" FF reed, place about 4 of them as separators and weave 3 more rows of 3/16" FO weaving the 12th row same as the 11th.
7. Start the next row behind a stake next to the handle weaving around with 3/16" FO reed
8. and ending behind the stake just before the opp handle stake. Repeat on opposite side.
9. Weave 4 more rows with 3/16 " FO reed stopping and starting one spoke farther from the handle stake on each row.
10. Tuck the center stakes on each side and trim the other stakes so there is a curved edge.
11. Using 3/8" FO reed for inner and outer rims (cut pieces at handles) and #8 round reed for filler, lash with 11/64" FO reed.
12. Lay two pieces of #3 round reed on handle and wrap with 3/16" FO reed. Start by wrapping over the round reed 2 times. Then go once under and twice over the rest of the way.
13. After staining, weave a ribbon or fabric through the 1" space after the 11 rows of 3/16" FO.

Elegant Storage Basket

Materials:
10x10 flat top D handle
¼" FO reed
3/8" FF reed
½" FF reed
5/8" FF reed
#2 round reed
#3 round reed, nat.
#3 round reed, dyed
#4 round reed

Cutting:
Cut 5 spokes of 5/8" FF reed 26" long
Cut 6 spokes of 3/8" FF reed 26" long
Cut 4 pieces of #4 round reed for locked coil.
Cut 24 pieces of #3 round reed 45" long for rim.
Cut 16 pieces of #3 round reed 28" long for lid.

Weaving:
1. Mark centers of all 5/8" FF spokes and mark 2" on each side of center on rough side. Mark centers of 3/8" FF spokes on rough side.
2. Mark center of handle. Lay 5/8" spokes on center alternating right and left with last spoke crossing handle at a right angle.
3. Bend a piece of #3 round reed. Begin twining at the 2" mark on one of the spokes and twine a circle at the 2" marks. Continue twining until you can get 2 fingers between spokes. (approx. 10 rows)
4. Add a 3/8" spoke to the right of the #1 spoke. Twine around it and the next 5/8" spoke. Add a new 3/8" spoke and continue in this manner until all 3/8" spokes are added. Twine until base measures 10". Cut weavers.
5. Bend spokes up.
6. With 4 pieces of #4 round reed, work a 4-rod locked coil:
    a) Insert a #4 round reed weaver behind spoke #1 and the next 3 spokes.
    b) Bring the left spoke in front of three spokes, behind one and out. Continue to spoke #1.
    c) Work a step-up--bring the left weaver in front of 3 spokes and behind one. Lift the original weaver and go under it and out to lock the coil. Repeat with 3, 2 and 1.
    d) Tighten by pulling ends in opposite directions. Cut ends with a slant so that they lied flush against the other weavers.
7. With #3 round reed, triple weave 4 rows.
8. Weave 5 rows with ¼" FO weaving first row over handle.
9. With dyed #3 reed, weave a row of twined arrows:
    a) With 2 pieces of reed, twine once around the basket.
    b) When you get to spoke #1, lift the right weaver and go under it with the left weaver, then behind and out. Continue in this manner.
    c) End the row by slipping the weaver under the beginning of the 2nd row.
10. Weave 1 row of 1" ash strip going over handle.

11. Weave another row of twined arrows.
12. Weave 2 rows of ¼" FO reed.
13. Weave 1 row of ½" FF reed.
14. Twine 3 rows of #3 round reed.
15. Trim and tuck spokes.
16. Work a rewoven braided border:
    a) Insert the 45" pieces of well-soaked round reed under the 3 rows of twining.
    b) Form scallops by inserting ends of pieces under twining of the 2nd spoke to the right.
    c) Start with any pair of round reed pieces and take them behind the pair to the right and out.
    d) Take a pair and go under only the pair to the right and up so that you don't go inside. Do this very loosely or the next row will be too tight.
    e) Each pair must now trace the path of the pair to the right. First, it will go down to the outside and then to the inside. The braid should stand up straight and not lean in.
17. The #3 round reed pairs on the inside will form spokes to make a lip for the basket. Using #2 round reed, twine 6 rows keeping spokes parallel to the base.
18. Use remaining length of spokes to make a simple braided border:
    a) Take a pair of spokes, go under 2 pairs to the right and up.
    b) Take a pair of spokes, go over two and to the inside.

Lid:
19. Soak the 28" lengths of #3 round reed and mark centers.
20. Group them into four groups of 4 and arrange them on a flat surface with 2 groups horizontal and 2 groups vertical overlapping as illustrated at right
21. Form pairs of spokes by pairing 1A and 1B, 2A and 2B, 3A and 3B, 4A and 4B. With 3 weavers of #3 round reed, triple weave pairing remaining groups similarly and forming a 4½" circle. Triple weave for 6 rows. Push center up to dome.
22. Separate the pairs and treat spokes individually for remainder of lid. With 2 pieces of dyed #3, weave 1 row of twined arrows.
23. With #3 round reed, triple weave until lid is about 9½" in diameter.
24. Border:
    a) With top of lid facing you, take any spoke, go behind 2 to the right and out.
    b) Weave 1 row of over 1 spoke and down.

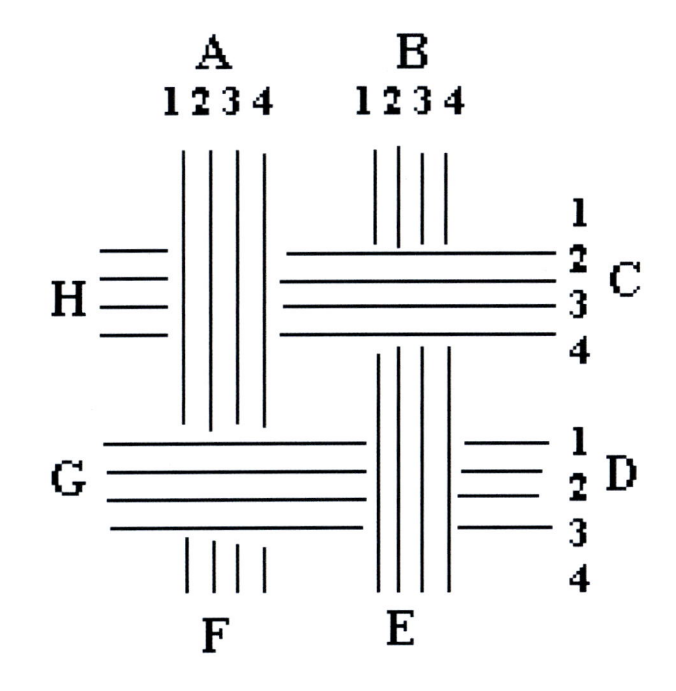

Big Bowl Basket

Materials:
14" round wood base
#3 round reed
¼" FO reed
½" FF reed
5/8" FF reed
5/8" FO reed
Sea grass

Cutting:
Cut 39 stakes of ¾" FF reed 11" long

Weaving:
1. Insert stakes evenly in base.
2. Twine 1 rows of #3 round reed.
3. Bend stakes up.
4. Beginning and ending with tapered ends and using ½" FF reed, weave 12 continuous rows flaring out slightly followed by 2 rows pulling in a little.
5. Weave an additional row of ½" FF reed for false rim.
6. Trim and tuck.
7. Use 5/8" FF reed for inner rim and 5/8" FO reed for outer rim. Fill with sea grass and lash with ¼" FO reed.

Round Basket with Diagonal Rim

Materials:
6" round wood base
#2 round reed, smoked
#3 round reed
¼" FO reed, smoked
3/8" FF reed

Cutting:
Cut 28 stakes of ¼" FO reed smoked 10" long
Cut 28 pieces of #3 round reed 14" long

Weaving:
1. Insert the stakes evenly in the base.
2. Twine 1 row with #2 round reed smoked.
3. Tapering the end of a piece of ¼" FO smoked reed, weave continuously 15 rows. Taper the end above the beginning taper. Diameter should be about 8".
4. Weave 1 row of 3/8" FF reed.
5. Weave continuously 4 rows of ¼" FO reed smoked tapering as above.
6. Triple twine 1 row with #3 round reed.
7. Twine 6 rows with #2 round reed doing stepups.
8. Trim and tuck all stakes.
9. Insert a piece of #3 round reed beside each tucked stake. Glue in place.
10. Weave diagonal border as follows:
    a) Behind one and out.
    b) Diagonally down in front of two spokes and under the 6 rows of twining.
    c) Diagonally behind two spokes and up into the loops of the first row.
    d) In front of two spokes and in.
    e) Over two and down.

Round Basket with Double Strand Braided Handle

Materials:
6" round wood base
1/4" FF reed
1/4" FO reed
1/2" FF reed
5/8" FF reed
7/8" FF reed
3/16" FO smoked reed
1/4" FF smoked reed
#2 round reed
#5 round reed

Cutting:
Cut 22 pieces of 5/8" FF reed 9 1/2" long
Cut 2 pieces of 7/8" FF reed 9 1/2" long

Weaving:
1. Insert the 24 cut pieces into base with the 7/8" pieces directly opposite each other.
2. Weave 4 rows #2 round reed.
3. Bend stakes up and weave 1 row 1/2" FF reed.
4. Weave 3 rows 1/4" FF smoked reed.
5. Weave 4 rows 1/2" FF reed.
6. Weave 3 rows 1/4" FF smoked reed.
7. Weave 4 rows 1/2" FF reed.
8. Trim and tuck
9. Cut a piece of 7/8" FF reed 16" long for handle.
10. Bend the ends of the handle and hook it under the false rim lining it up with the two 7/8" stakes.
11. Use 5/8" FF reed for inner and outer rims and #5 reed for filler.
12. Lash with 3/16" FO smoked reed.
13. Cut another piece of 7/8" FF reed and clip to underside of handle going from rim to rim.
14. Lay a piece of 1/4" FF reed on top of handle anchoring only the end where wrapping will begin. Always wrap over it in the remaining steps.
15. Mark handle 1 1/2" up from each end and wrap handle with 1/4" FO reed to the mark.
16. Cut 2 pieces of 1/4" FF smoked reed making each 5 times the distance between the marks.
17. Insert one piece of 1/4" smoked reed horizontally under the 1/4" vertical strip and wrap two times.
18. Insert the other piece of smoked reed horizontally and wrap two times.
19. Make an "X" with the smoked reed closest to the rim by crossing the left end over the 1/4" vertical piece and then pulling it under the vertical piece and out to the left. Pull taut. Do the same with the right end reversing directions.
20. Wrap 2 times.
21. Repeat step 19 with the second piece of smoked reed.

22. Continue the "X" pattern until you are 1/2" short of the mark on the opposite side of the handle.
23. Make an "X" as before and lay the ends flat on the handle. Wrap twice and repeat with other pieces.
24. Wrap down to the rim, trim smoked reed ends as you wrap.

Large Round Basket with Fabric and Notched Handle

Materials:
12" round notched handle with open notch
#2 round reed
#4 round reed
¼" FO reed
½" FF reed natural
½" FF reed dyed
5/8" FF reed
5/8" FO reed
Sea grass--#1 and #3
Fabric—1 strip 3-3¼" x 140"

Cutting:
Cut 8 pieces ½" FF reed natural 27" long
Cut 8 pieces ½" FF reed dyed 27" long

Weaving:
1. Lay 2 dyed pieces one on top of the other at 90 degree angles. Lay two other dyed pieces on top of them at 90 degrees to each other and 45 degrees to the original pieces.
2. Beginning 1" from the center, twine with #2 round reed 4 rows. (Diameter 4")
3. Lay 4 more dyed stakes between original stakes and continue twining 7 more rows. (Diameter 8")
4. Add 8 natural stakes and twine 5 or 6 rows — until diameter is 11".
5. Flip basket over and triple rod wale with #4 round reed.
6. Flip back to original position and bend stakes upward.
7. Weave 8 rows ¼" FO reed.
8. Add 3 continuous rows of fabric wrapping it with #1 sea grass around every other stake.
9. Weave 8 rows ¼" FO reed.
10. Weave 1 row ½" FF reed.
11. Insert hand behind the second row above fabric and several rows below.
12. Use 5/8" FF reed for inner rim and 5/8" FO for outer rim. Fill with #3 sea grass.
13. Lash with ¼" FO reed.

Round Gathering Basket

Materials:
10" round notched handle
#2 round reed
11/64" FO reed
3/16" FO reed
¼" FF reed space-dyed
3/8" FF reed
½" FF reed
½" FO reed
¾" FF reed, natural or dyed
sea grass

Cutting:
Cut 12 spokes ¾" FF reed, natural or dyed 23" long

Weaving:
1. Lay 6 of the spokes wrong side up in a circle. Crisscross them, don't go in order.
2. With #2 round reed, chase weave to a diameter of 6".
3. Lay the remaining 6 spokes on top and crisscross them.
4. Weave a row of 11/64" FO reed. When you get back to the beginning, shadow weave for several spokes and then go over two spokes and weave continuously for a total of 3 rows.
5. Cut all spokes in half lengthwise to the weavers except for one which will be cut into 3 to make an odd number.
6. Taper the last 3" of the next weaver (11/64" FO). Begin weaving in the spoke that was cut in three and weave continuously until base is 10" in diameter. End where you began with a tapered end.
7. Bend spokes upward.
8. Taper the end of a piece of space-dyed ¼" reed and weave over 2, under 1 continuously until the basket is 4 ½" high.
9. Weave a row of 3/8" FF reed.
10. Trim and tuck.
11. Use ½" FF reed for the inner rim and ½" FO reed for the outer rim. Fill with sea grass.
12. Push handle under inner rim on opposite sides.
13. Lash with 3/16" FO reed.

Round Gathering Basket with Wood Base

Materials:
10" round wood base
10" round notched handle with ends cut off ¼"
#2 round reed
¼" FO reed
¼" FF reed, dyed or space-dyed
½" FF reed
5/8" FF reed
5/8" FO reed
sea grass

Cutting:
Cut 40 stakes of ½" FF reed 7" long

Weaving:
1. Insert stakes evenly around base.
2. Twine 1 row with #2 round reed.
3. Bend stakes up.
4. Taper the end of a piece of ¼" dyed or space-dyed reed and weave over 2, under 1 continuously until the basket is 4 ½" high.
5. Weave a row of 3/8" FF reed for false rim.
6. Trim and tuck.
7. Use 5/8" FF reed for inner rim and 5/8" reed for outer rim. Fill with sea grass.
8. Push handle under inner rim on opposite sides. (Handle may need to be trimmed ¼" on ends.)
9. Lash with ¼" FO reed.

Beaded Basket

Materials:
6" square wood base with 32 holes
#3 round reed
#4 round reed
1/4" FO reed
96 pony beads

Cutting:
Cut 32 spokes of #4 round reed 20" long

Weaving:
1. Insert 1 spoke into each hole of wood base. Leave about 3" extending below the bottom.
2. To weave the bottom, select any reed and weave it behind the spoke on the right (inside basket), in front of the next two spokes (outside) and behind the next spoke. Repeat this around the base.
3. Triple weave 5 rows using #3 round reed weaving continuously.
4. Weave 11 rows of 1/4" FO reed making sure that the first row is outside the corner spokes.
5. Triple twine 2 rows using #3 round reed.
6. Add beads as follows: 4 beads on center spokes, 3 on next spokes right and left, then 2 and then 1. (No beads on corner spokes.)
7. Triple twine 2 rows of #3 round reed bending sides out.
8. Place 1 bead on each spoke.
9. Triple twine 4 rows of #3 round reed continuing to bend out.
10. Braid border as follows:
    - Selecting any 2 spokes, bend the left spoke behind the right spoke (inside the basket) and then bring it to the outside. Continue this to the right around the basket.
    - Select 3 spokes, bend the left spoke to the right (outside the basket) in front of the other 2 spokes and then to the inside, inserting it in the hole to the right of the third spoke.
    - For the last row, working inside the basket, select 3 spokes, bring the left one over the two to the right and then bend it down.
11. After basket is thoroughly dry, cut off the excess spoke length.

Oval Basket with Beads

Materials:
4" x 8" oval wood base
¼" FF reed
3/8" FF reed
½" FF reed
¾" FF reed
11/64" FO reed
½" FO reed
#2 round reed
#5 round reed
24" beaded fringe

Cutting:
Cut 24 stakes ½" FF reed 7 ½" long

Weaving:
1. Insert stakes evenly in base.
2. Twine 2 rows with #2 round reed.
3. Bend stakes up.
4. Weave 2 rows with ¼" FF reed.
5. Triple twine 2 rows with #2 round reed.
6. Weave 1 row with ¾" FF reed.
7. Triple twine 2 rows with #2 round reed.
8. Weave 13 rows ¼" FF reed.
9. Weave false rim with 3/8" FF reed.
10. Trim and tuck.
11. Glue fringe tape to false rim.
12. Use ½" FF reed for inner rim, ½" FO reed for outer rim, fill with #5 round reed and lash with 11/64" FO reed.

Multi-Color Bowl Basket

Materials:
6" round wood base
#2 round reed
¼" FO reed
¼" FF reed, nat.
¼" FF reed, dyed
3/8" FF reed
3/8" FO reed
3/16" FO reed
sea grass for filler

Cutting:
Cut 28 pieces 3/8" FF reed 8" long
Cut 28 pieces of ¼" FF reed dyed in an
　　assortment of colors 7" long

Weaving:
1. Insert the 28 – 3/8" stakes evenly around the base.
2. Chase weave 3 rows of round reed.
3. Weave 6 rows of ¼" FO reed lifting each row so that the stakes are almost vertical after 6 rows. (Diameter approx. 8 ¼" - 8 ½")
4. Triple weave 2 rows with round reed.
5. Weave the 28 dyed pieces of ¼" FF reed diagonally.
6. Triple weave 2 rows with round reed.
7. Weave 3 rows ¼" FO reed.
8. Weave 1 row ¼" FF reed for false rim.
9. Use 3/8" FF reed for inner rim, 3/8" FO reed for outer rim and sea grass for filler.
10. Lash with 3/16" FO reed.

Pitcher Basket #1

Materials:
4 ½" wood base
#2 round reed
3/16" FO reed
¼" FF reed
3/8" FF reed
3/8" FO reed
½" FF reed
½" FO reed
sea grass

Cutting:
Cut 19 stakes of 3/8" FF reed 14" long
Cut 1 handle stake of ½" FF reed 30" long

A B

Weaving:
Note: Instructions are for basket A shown on left. Changes in brackets are for basket B shown on right.

1. Insert all 20 stakes into wood base.
2. Chase weave twice around base with #2 round reed. DO NOT CUT.
3. Bend stakes gently upward.
4. Add a third piece of #2 round reed and triple weave three rows.
5. Begin weaving with ¼" FF reed with the first row going over the handle stake. Weave 19 [26] rows altogether flaring outward slightly. [Pull in after the 20th row.]
6. Weave 1 row of 3/8" FF reed.
7. Twine 7 [4] rows with #2 round reed pulling in to taper the shape of the pitcher.
8. [Basket A only: Weave 5 rows of ¼" FF reed making sure to go under the handle stake on the first and last rows and pulling tight to continue the inward shaping of the pitcher].
9. Start the next row behind the spoke next to the handle spoke. Weave around with ¼" FF reed and end behind the spoke next to the handle spoke on the other side.
10. Weave 8 more rows with ¼" FF reed stopping and starting one spoke further from the handle spoke and pushing outward to form pouring spout.
11. Weave a false rim row of ¼" FF reed.
12. Complete handle:
    - Insert end of handle spoke under the weavers in rows 13, 15 and 17.
    - Trim to desired length, bend end up about ¾" and insert under the weaver in row 15.
    - Cut a piece of ½" FO reed a little longer than the handle.
    - Place flat side of FO piece on outside of handle and tuck ends under weavers at both ends.
    - Wrap handle with ¼" FF reed.
13. Trim and tuck spokes.
14. Using 3/8" FO reed for inner and outer rims, fill with sea grass and lash with 3/16" FO reed.

Pitcher Basket #2

Materials:
4 ½" wood base
#2 round reed
3/16" FO reed
¼" FF reed
3/8" FF reed
3/8" FO reed
½" FF reed
½" FO reed
5/8" FF reed dyed
sea grass

Cutting:
Cut 19 stakes 3/8" FF reed 16" long
Cut 1 handle stake of ½" FF reed 30" long

Weaving:
1. Insert all 20 stakes into wood base.
2. Twine two rows around base with #2 round reed. DO NOT CUT.
3. Bend stakes gently upward.
4. Add a third piece of #2 round reed and triple weave three rows doing a step-up on each row.
5. Begin weaving with ¼" FF reed with the first row going over the handle stake. Weave 11 rows altogether flaring outward. Diameter should be about 7.5 ".
6. Weave 1 row of sea grass, 1 row of dyed 5/8" FF reed, and 1 row of sea grass.
7. Weave 5 more rows of ¼" FF reed. Diameter should be slightly more than 8".
8. Bend stakes in slightly and weave 1 more row of ¼" FF reed.
9. With #2 round reed, triple twine 7 rows with step-ups pulling in to a diameter of about 6.5".
10. Weave 13 more rows of ¼" FF reed with the first row going under the handle stake. Pull in for the first 10 rows and then begin flaring out.
11. Start the next row behind the spoke next to the handle spoke. Weave around with ¼ " FF reed and end behind the spoke next to the handle spoke on the other side.
12. Weave 8 more rows with ¼ " FF reed stopping and starting one spoke further from the handle spoke and pushing outward to form pouring spout. Leave long ends on these pieces.
13. Weave a false rim row of ¼" FF reed.
14. Complete handle:
    a) Determine desired length of handle, bend end to the inside and insert under the 3rd and 5th rows of ¼" reed above the sea grass.
    b) Trim the end so that there is about ½" above the 5th row of ¼" reed.
    c) Cut a piece of ½" FO reed a little longer than the handle and taper both ends.
    d) Place flat side of FO piece on outside of handle and tuck ends under weavers at both ends.
    e) Wrap handle with ¼" FF reed.
15. Trim and tuck spokes.
16. Using 3/8" FO for outer rim and 3/8" FF for inner rim, fill with sea grass and lash with 3/16" FO reed.

Bowl Basket

Materials:
6" round wood base
#2 round reed
3/16" FO reed
¼" FF reed
3/8" FF reed
3/8" FO reed
5/8" FF reed dyed
sea grass

Cutting:
Cut 28 stakes of 3/8" FF reed 9" long

Weaving:
1. Insert the 28 stakes evenly around the base.
2. With #2 round reed, twine 9 rows around the base pulling up gradually to begin bowl shape.
3. Weave 9 rows of ¼" FF reed pulling in to continue bowl shape.
4. Weave 1 row of sea grass, 1 row 5/8" FF dyed reed, and 1 row of sea grass.
5. With #2 reed, triple twine 14 rows. The first 7 rows should go up continuing the bowl shape. Then begin rolling the rim out and down for the next 7 rows.
6. Weave a false rim row of ¼" FF reed.
7. Trim the stakes that are under the false rim even with the edge of the rim. Trim the stakes on the outside to about ¾", bend the under the false rim and clip them.
8. Use 3/8" FO reed for the outside rim and 3/8" FF reed for the under rim. Lash with 3/16" FO reed.

Small Pitcher Basket

Materials:
4" round wood base
11/64" FO reed
¼" FF reed
¼" FO reed smoked
7mm FF reed
3/8" FF reed
3/8" FO reed
#2 round reed
Sea grass

Cutting:
Cut 19 stakes of 3/8' FF reed 10" long
Cut 1 stake of ½" FF reed 10" long
Cut 1 piece of ½" FF reed 20" long for handle

Weaving:
1. Insert stakes evenly in base. (The ½" stake is for the handle placement.)
2. Weave 2 rows of 11/64" FO reed. On the 1st row weave outside the handle. On the second row begin lifting slightly.
3. Weave 8 rows of 7mm FF reed bringing basket to a diameter of 5-5.5".
4. Insert the 20" piece of ½" FF reed under the 5th and 7th 7mm weavers from the top.
5. Taper the ends of a piece of ¼' FO smok reed and twill (over 2, under 1) weave continuously for 7 rows.
6. Weave 6 rows of 7 mm reed (first row over the handle) pulling in.
7. Separate 20" handle stake from the original stake and weave 2 more rows of 7 mm excluding handle.
8. Bend stakes out slightly and weave 2 more rows of 7 mm reed flaring out.
9. Mark the stake opp the handle stake.
10. Cut 6 pieces of 7mm reed 14", 12", 10", 8", 6", 4". Beginning at the center stake (opp handle) weave each of these in order from bottom to top pulling out to make a pouring spout. Leave ends on the inside and DO NOT CUT.
11. Weave 1 row of 7 mm FF for false rim.
12. Trim and tuck the stakes and then cut the ends of the weavers so that they will be hidden under the rim.
13. Use 3/8" FF reed for inner rim and 3/8" FO for outer rim, fill with sea grass and lash with 11/64" FO.
14. Handle: Bend the 20" handle piece down and push it from the top under the 5th and 7th rows pulling it to desired length. Bend it at the bottom and push it in at the top under the 5th, 3rd, and 1st rows so that the handle is double.
15. Wrap the handle with ¼" FF reed.

Made in the USA
Columbia, SC
09 March 2023